101 Museum Programs Under $100

Proven Programs That Work on a Shoestring Budget

Lauren E. Hunley

American Association for State and Local History

ROWMAN & LITTLEFIELD
Lanham • Boulder • New York • London

AMERICAN ASSOCIATION FOR STATE AND LOCAL HISTORY BOOK SERIES

ABOUT THE SERIES

The American Association for State and Local History book series addresses issues critical to the field of state and local history through interpretive, intellectual, scholarly, and educational texts. To submit a proposal or manuscript to the series, please request proposal guidelines from AASLH headquarters: AASLH Editorial Board, 2021 21st Ave. South, Suite 320, Nashville, Tennessee 37212. Telephone: (615) 320-3203. Website: www.aaslh.org.

ABOUT THE ORGANIZATION

The American Association for State and Local History (AASLH) is a national history membership association headquartered in Nashville, Tennessee, that provides leadership and support for its members who preserve and interpret state and local history in order to make the past more meaningful to all people. AASLH members are leaders in preserving, researching, and interpreting traces of the American past to connect the people, thoughts, and events of yesterday with the creative memories and abiding concerns of people, communities, and our nation today. In addition to sponsorship of this book series, AASLH publishes *History News* magazine, a newsletter, technical leaflets and reports, and other materials; confers prizes and awards in recognition of outstanding achievement in the field; supports a broad education program and other activities designed to help members work more effectively; and advocates on behalf of the discipline of history. To join AASLH, go to www.aaslh.org or contact Membership Services, AASLH, 2021 21st Ave. South, Suite 320, Nashville, TN 37212.

Published by Rowman & Littlefield
A wholly owned subsidiary of The Rowman & Littlefield Publishing Group, Inc.
4501 Forbes Boulevard, Suite 200, Lanham, Maryland 20706
www.rowman.com

Unit A, Whitacre Mews, 26-34 Stannary Street, London SE11 4AB

British Library Cataloguing in Publication Information Available

Library of Congress Cataloging-in-Publication Data Available
Library of Congress Control Number: 2018949028

ISBN 978-1-5381-0302-9 (cloth : alk. paper)
ISBN 978-1-5381-0303-6 (pbk. : alk. paper)
ISBN 978-1-5381-0304-3 (electronic)

♾™ The paper used in this publication meets the minimum requirements of
American National Standard for Information Sciences—Permanence of Paper
for Printed Library Materials, ANSI/NISO Z39.48-1992.

Printed in the United States of America

Contents

List of Figures and Tables   vii

Preface   ix

Acknowledgments   xiii

1 Programming for Today   1

2 Programming for Children and Families   9

3 Programming for Teens and Young Adults   65

4 Programming for Adults   91

5 Programming for Multigenerational   113

6 Adapting, Expanding, and Implementing Museum
   Programs   157

Appendix A Project Contributors   163

Appendix B Program Planning Checklist   169

Appendix C Developing a Museum Program: Sample
            Program Planning Worksheet   171

Appendix D Developing a Museum Program: Blank
            Program Planning Worksheet   173

Index   175

About the Author   181

List of Figures and Tables

FIGURES

1.1	Museum Ideological Structure	3
1.2	Program or Exhibit: Comparing Museum Components	4
2.1	Hashnife Pony Express Arrival	17
2.2	Pop-Up Make 'n' Take	20
2.3	President's Day Event with Congressman Jim Jordan	21
2.4	Start with Art	23
2.5	Stories on the Staircase	25
2.6	Special Nights for Special Needs	27
2.7	Preschool Story Time	28
2.8	Neighborhoods	32
2.9	Pioneer Garden	34
2.10	Artifact Detective and Exhibit Label Workshop	37
2.11	Children's Battle of Lexington Reenactment	38
2.12	Summer STEAM: Signal Flags and Semaphore	40
2.13	Youth Tour Ambassadors	41
2.14	Sewing and Circuits	47
2.15	Canning Creations	49
2.16	First Fridays	51
2.17	Playdate: Happy Birthday Trees!	54
2.18	Gold Panning	55
2.19	Victorian Christmas	58
2.20	Kids Dig	60
2.21	Mornings at the Museum	61
2.22	Lulie Crawford Wildflowers and Watercolors	63
3.1	Snapchat	69
3.2	Student Choice	71
3.3	Tumblr	72
3.4	Teen Summer Internships	76
4.1	Palisades Mill: From Wool to Whalers	88

4.2	History Club	91
4.3	Evening at the Museum	93
4.4	Discovering History through Artifacts	96
4.5	Behind the Velvet Ropes	99
4.6	SPARK! Cultural Programming for People with Memory Loss	105
4.7	Unlocking the Stories	108
4.8	Father's Day Beer Talk and Tasting	110
4.9	History Happy Hour	112
5.1	Spycast	118
5.2	Japanese Name Interpretation Workshop	120
5.3	Poetry 'n' Rhythm	121
5.4	Twilight Tours	123
5.5	Meet the Artist	128
5.6	Baldwin Home Candlelight Tour	130
5.7	Echoes of the Past Cemetery Tours	132
5.8	Museum Collection Protection: Gallery Cleaning	134
5.9	Shovel Ready	136
5.10	Art with Emotion	137
5.11	Stars and Stardust: Sidewalk Astronomy in the Neon Boneyard	139
5.12	Fossil Dig	140
5.13	Learning about *Your* Past	141
5.14	Panel Discussion on Race and Ethnicity	143
5.15	Thursday Night Lineup	144
5.16	How to Make Hypertufa Pots	146
5.17	Hands-On History Carts	149
5.18	Veterans Day Program	152
5.19	Yule Log Hunt	155

TABLE

P.1	Program Types by Chapter	x–xi

Preface

The 2016–2017 fiscal year hit my museum pretty hard. We saw a 52 percent cut to our staff, and our operations dwindled to necessary expenses only. As the education department head, I found many of my established programs put on hold due to lack of resources. I realized that, to continue hosting museum programs, I would have to get creative and do so for—as my boss said—"nothing." I began looking for other innovative and inexpensive museum programs to adapt, and the deeper I looked, the more I realized a few things: (1) Museum professionals are creative, resourceful, and innovative. We do so much with so little; and (2) I couldn't be the only one looking for these types of programs. Thus, *101 Museum Programs Under $100* was born.

Numerous museums across the country have found programmatic success with minimal financial investments. Many of these programs are outlined in the following pages. They are as varied in type as they are in scope, but they are all included because of one simple requirement: they are produced for $100 or less. More than 380 different museums were encouraged to share their programs, not only their planning outlines, but also the feasibility of duplicating them at other facilities. Seventy-four museums responded with 101 programs (see appendix A for a full participant list). While some of these programs are similar in approach or design, each includes unique components that are integral to their success.

UNDERSTANDING THIS RESOURCE AND HOW TO USE IT

Each program included has details on the type of museum hosting it, the target audience, and its attendance. Programs' interpretive components, audience time requirements, ease of scaling to a smaller or larger audience (scalability), and budget are also discussed. While the budget listed does not include staff time or marketing costs, staff time requirements are also included in each program listing. Staff costs are true costs that should be considered, but they are not factored into these budget descriptions because these costs are highly variable across museums. Including these costs would require knowledge of staff wages and salaries, which is individually based on experience and museum operation budgets. Many museums even depend heavily on volunteers, sometimes bringing this financial cost to zero.

Marketing costs are not included for similar reasons. Many museums have a separate budgetary line for marketing costs, so they are often not factored into programming expenses. Also, museums are able to take advantage of many marketing opportunities that have little overhead. These options are discussed in chapter 1, "Programming for Today."

When considering the ratings for interpretive components and scalability, it is important to note that these are not grades. Instead, they highlight the amount of involvement and work each program requires. Interpretive components include the ease of sharing interpretation in the program design, the amount of interpretation able to be shared, and whether the information could be personalized for the audience. For scalability, flexibility of event location and the amount of staff time and resources required to scale it are considered.

Each entry also includes a brief analysis that highlights the unique program aspects that set it apart from other similar programs. Additionally, this analysis section often contains further information on how other museums could feasibly replicate that program. This replicability was more difficult to ascertain because of the unknown nature of resource availability at other museums, but certain programming aspects can still be brought to the fore for consideration.

To help make these programs easy to find and use, they are organized by audience type and then by budget requirement. This allows programs to be browsed and selected based on what best fits a museum's needs (see table P.1). This information provides the foundation necessary to adapt programming components to other facilities. A more detailed discussion on how to adapt and implement museum programs is included in chapter 6, "Adapting, Expanding, and Implementing Museum Programs."

Table P.1. Program types by chapter

Program Types	Chapter 2: Children and Families	Chapter 3: Teens and Young Adults	Chapter 4: Adults	Chapter 5: Multi-generational Audiences
Activity-Based	2	1	—	1
Community Exhibit	1	—	—	3

Contest	—	1	—	—
Demonstration	—	—	—	3
Event	5	—	3	5
In-Gallery	8	—	1	3
Lecture	—	—	4	1
Off-Site	1	—	1	3
Open House	6	—	4	3
Oral History	—	—	2	—
Partnership	10	1	6	5
Podcast	—	—	—	1
School	6	2	—	—
Social Club	1	1	3	1
Social Media	—	2	—	—
Story Time	4	—	—	—
Tour	1	3	4	6
Volunteer	1	3	—	—
Workshop	6	1	5	6

Note: Amounts total more than 101, as some programs fall under multiple categories.

CHAPTER BREAKDOWNS

These chapters are intended to ease the process of conceptualizing and creating successful museum programs. Each chapter breaks the scope and scale into manageable pieces. Chapter 1 explores what constitutes a museum program and its various pieces; it also includes a note on successful marketing in the digital age. Chapter 2 highlights 37 programs targeting children and accompanying adults. Chapter 3 includes 10 programs for teenagers and young adults. Chapter 4 breaks down 23 programs designed for adult-only audiences, and chapter 5 outlines 31 programs for multigenerational audiences (or groups with multiple generations represented). This overview concludes in chapter 6 with a discussion of how to adapt and implement museum programs for other organizations.

I hope that *101 Museum Programs under $100* jump-starts new programming ideas while exploring the innovative and unique museum programs already in use across the country. These programs are working in their respective organizations, and they're flourishing with little financial buy-in. May you be just as successful. Good luck.

Acknowledgments

This book would not be possible without the love and support of my friends, colleagues, family, and God and—perhaps just as important—without the museums who've shared their programming details with this project. A publication like this cannot happen with one person's research and input. Each museum took the time to share program details, challenges, and photographs, and their willingness shows. To list everyone and what they meant would take dozens of pages to express (for a full list of participating museums, see appendix A).

Special thanks to my editor, Charles Harmon, who helped guide this process, to Kristin and Nicholas for their first look and input, and to my family for supporting me throughout this work.

1

Programming for Today

Museum professionals break the mold on innovating under limitations. In a world of increasing responsibilities, expanding programming challenges, shrinking staffs, and declining budgets, we continue to implement dynamic, engaging programs that draw and inspire our audiences. To do this, we get creative in our resourcefulness. *Recycle, upcycle, bargain hunting*, and *do-it-yourself* are not just buzzwords for us. They are ever-present realities of operating in today's museum field.

Museum programs deepen audience involvement. Everyone loves the bells and whistles of those institutional programs with staff and resources available to outfit an immersive visitor experience. Programs like the National Constitution Center's video-supplemented, theatrical *Freedom Rising* in Philadelphia, Pennsylvania, are impressive in their implementation and intimidating in their scope. But let's be realistic. How many institutions can plan on that scale? Fifty-seven percent of museums in the United States operate on a $130,000 budget (or less) and have a staff of three or fewer.[1] Million-dollar programs are not in our organizational capabilities.

But we are adaptive museum professionals. We are prolific in the "just make it work" business model, and there is so much we can learn from each other. When it comes to museum programming, we can take a page from Minnesota senator Paul Wellstone's book. He said, "We all do better when we all do better,"[2] and armed with the successes (and failures) of our fellow museum associates, we are better able to design, implement, and manage realistic museum programs for all our audiences. Let's face it. It's easy to get so bogged down in daily operations and budget limitations that we can't see the programming opportunities right in front of us. Being open to new sources of inspiration provides fresh perspectives and boosts our own innovative possibilities.

WHAT IS A MUSEUM PROGRAM?

Museum programming covers a wide range of museum operations. Gallery activities, special events, site tours, and classroom presentations all fall under this vague categorization. But how do we define *museum program* beyond the ambiguous "you know it when you see it"?

When we boil down the components of a museum program, we get a few consistent key identifiers:

- It's scheduled, whether regularly (e.g., weekly, monthly), periodically (e.g., annually), or by appointment.
- It's designed for museum audience consumption.
- It's led by museum representatives, whether paid staff or volunteer.

To put it plainly, a museum program is a scheduled, audience-centered, mission-based, interpretive activity facilitated by museum representatives. All programs have these components. However, truly successful, memorable programs boast a few additional elements.

WHAT IS A MUSEUM PROGRAM?

A museum program is a scheduled, audience-centered, mission-based, interpretive activity facilitated by museum representatives.

Museum programming must be mission driven. Our exhibits, events, branding, and programming should make sense to who we are, what we do, and what we want to accomplish. In short, it must fit our mission.

An organizational mission defines why the organization exists, its goals, and its desired outputs. The vision statement alludes to the type of future the organization works toward. Mission-based programming garners support for this vision, the organization, and the museum collection. This aid can take the format of volunteers, financial contributions, or political support and must be oriented toward the organization's mission and vision. Imagine the organization as a building. The mission creates a strong foundation, and the programs and exhibits create the walls to hold up the roof, or the organization's vision (see figure 1.1). Without the foundation, it crumbles; without the walls, there is no building. If the program does not grow from the mission and uphold the vision, then it should be reconsidered. Keeping it can create confusion and distract your audience, your community, and your staff.

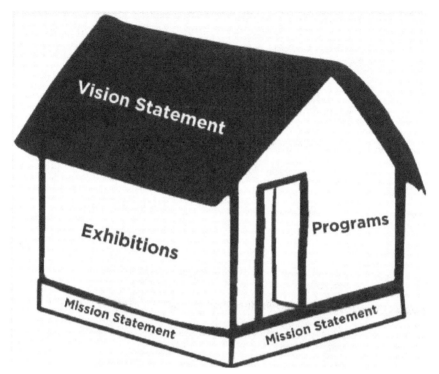

Figure 1.1 Like a building's walls, museum programs and exhibits should build upon the organization's mission toward its vision.

Museum programming must be interpretive. Part of a museum's most basic function is as an educational organization. Everything a museum does is centered on preserving and sharing the unique stories associated with its collection. Museums are in the singular position to reflect on cultural conventions in society by connecting authentic objects to personal human stories. As such, Americans see museums as one of the most trusted sources for objective information.[3] Our goal is to inform and educate while providing an enjoyable and thought-provoking experience. Programming supports this effort and increases the audience's ability to relate to, appreciate, and understand object stories and their relevance to audience lives.

The nature of a program comes down to the needs, resources, and limitations of the museum hosting it. While these challenges are perceived largely to be unique among organizations, we can draw encouragement in that we are not alone in our programming challenges. We can learn from other organizations. What works for them may very well work for us. While some museums have adequate classroom spaces, many are restricted to only exhibit and gallery spaces, and they use it well. Paint-based toddler studio classes may not be the best fit for museums with a predominately historic collection, but some facilities make it work. The trick is designing programs that fit your mission but equally appeal to your identified audience.

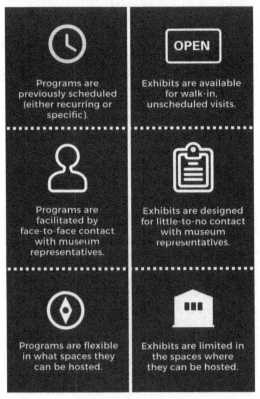

PROGRAM

OR

EXHIBIT

COMPARING MUSEUM COMPONENTS

Programs are previously scheduled (either recurring or specific).

Exhibits are available for walk-in, unscheduled visits.

Programs are facilitated by face-to-face contact with museum representatives.

Exhibits are designed for little-to-no contact with museum representatives.

Programs are flexible in what spaces they can be hosted.

Exhibits are limited in the spaces where they can be hosted.

Figure 1.2 Museum programs and exhibits are fundamentally different.

It is worth noting that museum programs and museum exhibits are not synonymous (see figure 1.2). Among other distinctions, exhibits are static and designed to serve the audience without direct interaction with museum representatives. Programs are dependent on this interaction. While both are essential to the function of a museum and they may relate to and be dependent on each other, they operate under different requirements and are managed separately.

A NOTE ON MARKETING IN THE DIGITAL AGE

There's a great program planned, but how do we get people to come? While the listed budgets in this publication do not include advertising costs, it is important to remember multiple marketing considerations during the planning process. Museum marketing is simply communicating the awesome things we're doing to the people who are ready to participate or perhaps even convincing them to do so. We must consider several essential elements of effective museum marketing:

- *Know who the audience is.* Are they a proven group who know and like you? Are they an as-yet-unserved group you would like to reach? Identify who the program is for before moving forward with an advertising plan.
- *Identify the best ways to talk to your audience.* Where do they go? Who do they talk to? How do they get their information? This differs based on the target audience's age, generation, socioeconomic situation, level of education, and even residence. Find out where they go, and talk to them there.
- *Faithfully evaluate all marketing efforts.* Is what you're doing working? Are you attracting the people you wanted or expected? Take surveys. Ask questions. Talk to people. Listen. And incorporate those answers into your next marketing plan.

Beyond these essentials, understanding how to market museum programs and events in the digital age can be confusing and overwhelming. With the rise of complex digital platforms like e-learning, massive open online courses (MOOCs), and seemingly innumerable social media outlets, you may be tempted to ignore the online world completely. On the flip side, with so many perceived "free and easy" options online, you might spend all your marketing resources there and eschew more traditional platforms. Both approaches would be a mistake. When planning a comprehensive marketing approach, it benefits to consider a few things:

- *Digital presence is key.* This means having an up-to-date website, active social media profiles, and responsive digital engagement. Chances are, before they participate in your program (or even walk through your museum doors), participants have already visited your website, checked when your last Facebook post was, and verified your rating on TripAdvisor, Yelp, and Google.

• *Recognize the strength (and weaknesses) of social media.* While Facebook, Twitter, Instagram, and other social media outlets have huge potential for marketing, simply making a post isn't enough. New algorithmic changes on these sites prevent all fans and followers from seeing your posts unless a paid "boost" or advertisement is secured. Instead, post distribution is based on follower engagement (e.g., likes, shares, comments). This requires posts that are intentionally designed to spark responses.

• *Don't overextend yourself.* It may be tempting to have multiple social media accounts to appeal to every online audience, but these accounts depend on frequent updates. Pick one or two that can be maintained on a daily basis, and do them well rather than trying to manage numerous accounts unsuccessfully.

• *Don't discount traditional print media.* Newspaper advertisements, posters in the library, and radio copy not only increase the visibility of your program but also solidify community relationships that will benefit your organization in the future.

• *Word of mouth can be your greatest asset.* Personal communications have long been the most consistent and most dependable marketing avenue, and now with the internet, individual users have the potential to reach thousands more. Encourage staff, board, volunteers, and previous participants to share the program both online and face-to-face.

Of course, half of the advertising battle is finding the resources to adequately market the program. Many of us do not have the luxury of a dedicated marketing budget and must find ways to carve funding from other places. This can be difficult, and few grants fund marketing costs. Luckily there are several low-cost or no-cost options. As previously mentioned, social media provides great benefits if leveraged correctly. Self-printed posters and postcard-sized ads work wonders when spread throughout a community (e.g., libraries, businesses, recreation centers), and press releases are an often-overlooked tool for free marketing. While sending a press release to local and regional media outlets does not guarantee their use, most local newspapers, magazines, and radio stations (especially in smaller communities) capitalize on the submission to develop their own news stories.

A final thought on marketing your program: Be bold. Seek partnerships in and around your community to cover your program's needs. Sometimes the unforeseen or unpredictable partnership will be the most beneficial. Working on a story time? Go to your library. Creating a special-needs activity? Pitch it to your local Veterans Affairs or special-needs organization. Showing a themed movie? Check out your local organizations with similar themed interests, such as the Elks Lodge or a local church. Such partnerships help pool resources for greater impact and can help your program and organization to reach new audiences.

Programs are the cornerstone for many museums in creating compelling and memorable experiences for their audiences, and we leverage our amazing talents to make them seemingly appear from nothing: no resources, little staff, and even less support. This book is for us. May our imagination run freely fueled by these new ideas.

NOTES

1 E-mail message to author from Alana Coleman, member services and registration manager, American Alliance of Museums, November 28, 2016.
2 Paul Wellstone, "Sheet Metal Workers Speech," September 1999, http://www.wellstone.org/legacy/speeches/sheet-metal-workers-speech.
3 Lake, Snell, Perry, and Associates, "Nationwide Public Opinion Survey," commissioned by the American Alliance of Museums, 2001.

2

Programming for Children and Families

For many museums, programs targeting children and their families are the first—and sometimes only—consideration for programming resources. For those in the museum field, this young audience constitutes future museumgoers, volunteers, and donors. Reaching them at an early age is paramount. So how can museums attract this audience and keep them invested?

For children and their families, museums offer a unique educational environment where learning happens through self-discovery in real-life settings. Familiar objects open windows to critical thinking exercises and new ideas, often without the child even being aware they're flexing these mental muscles.

From the museum's perspective, programs for children should be done on their level—cognitively, physically, and emotionally. This requires independent planning and unique program offerings. As Freeman Tilden, the noted pioneer in cultural and natural interpretation, stated, "Interpretation addressed to children should not be a dilution of the presentations to adults but should follow a fundamentally different approach." In other words, children's programming is not just a dumbed-down version of what their parents get. They have their own focus and goals.

When planning children's programs, museums should remember to focus on specific concepts through tactile and kinesthetic activities. A hands-on approach solidifies the child's grasp of concrete ideas and relates it back to their limited life experiences. Through interaction with museum representatives, children can become more engaged with the information, keeping their interest and curiosity.

SCHOOL PROGRAMS

Classroom groups can be a consistent and dedicated audience for museum programming efforts. Matching school curricula with museum themes seems fairly straightforward, but there are challenges associated with this targeted audience. While teachers can be an easy sell on the value of museum programs, their curricular and administrative requirements make it extremely difficult to fit such programs into their schedules. Limited funds and sifting through field trip options further add to the challenges of organizing student travel. The success of any program aimed at schools is dependent on whether the museum takes these factors into account. These programs should function within a limited time slot, even if the program must be split over multiple engagements. Programs like Neighborhoods at the Johnson County Jim Gatchell Memorial Museum and Artifact Detective at the Historical Museum at Fort Missoula spread components over two to three meetings to fit into tight school schedules and ensure full student understanding.

School programs should take a multidisciplinary approach to match the museum's interpretive goals with educators' learning standards. For example, history programs may incorporate math. Art discussions might include history, and both could find opportunities to touch on the science involved in each. Using museum collections to explore these varied topics can be both challenging and invigorating. Such programs as Start with Art at the Mabee-Gerrer Museum illustrate this programmatic success.

These programs should also strive for active student involvement to deepen understanding and application to classroom studies. This can be achieved through conversations and interactions, such as in the Daviess County Historical Society Museum's Fourth-Grade Trips, or it can involve the students in the stories told. Programs like Agecroft Hall's Voyage to Virginia and the Lexington Historical Society's Children's Battle of Lexington Reenactment actively draw student participants into the interpretation by assigning them roles and duties associated with the program content.

WORKSHOPS

Regularly scheduled workshops offer a great way to bring children and their families into the museum space. Hands-on, activity-based content shared among smaller groups encourages deeper engagement and comprehension. These workshops can cover any variety of topics, from traditional home crafts, like the Friends of the Pound House Foundation's Canning Creations, to field-specific investigations, like the Wyoming Dinosaur Center's Kids Dig. They can explore artistic expression, like the Tread of the Pioneers' Lulie Crawford Wildflowers and Watercolors program, and they can combine seemingly dissimilar concepts, such as the Cape Fear Museum's Sewing and Circuits. They can even draw families together through active collaboration, like the Evansville African American Museum's Family Painting Workshop. The possibilities for child-centered museum workshops are endless.

OPEN HOUSE

Open houses geared for child and family audiences offer great opportunities for museums to expose this audience to numerous fields, concepts, and activities without overwhelming them. Families are given the flexibility to explore at their pace, to visit areas that draw their attention, and to collaborate with each other throughout. These open-house events can be themed, like the Moody Museum's Victorian Christmas. They can open the museum space for an otherwise-underserved audience, like the Children's Museum of Richmond's Special Nights for Special Needs, and they can utilize community partnerships to expand audience exposure, like the Shenandoah Valley Discovery Museum's cooperation with Shenandoah University's nursing program to host their Healthy Fridays event. Open houses are a great way to give children and their families the freedom to explore museum offerings on their terms.

EVENTS

Major events offer the opportunity to explore mutually beneficial partnerships with community members and organizations. Sharing event responsibilities with another group extends museum exposure and resources. These partnerships can be with a formal organization, such as the Hashknife Pony Express Arrival hosted by the Western Spirit Museum and the Hashknife Pony Express organization, or they can work with a single individual with the ability to fulfill the museums' event needs. This can be seen in the Rutherford B. Hayes's President's Day Event with Congressman Jim Jordan. Congressman Jordan donates his time, the museum organizes the event, and the participating children benefit. While events can be time consuming and require a certain dedication to ensure success, seeking partnerships can greatly alleviate these challenges.

POP-UP PROGRAMS

Pop-up programs are activity-based programs that occur in spaces dedicated to other purposes. These programs can happen in galleries, open foyers, and even outside. They tend to have low staff time commitments and can be either regularly scheduled, like the Grace Museum's Pop-Up Make N' Take, or one-time events, like the National Mining Hall of Fame and Museum's Gold Panning activity. They usually have a small interpretive aspect that includes a craft or hands-on activity component. The US Naval Undersea Museum and Skirball Cultural Center both heavily used themed activities to engage their audiences with their planned interpretation in their Summer STEAM: Signal Flags and Semaphore and Playdate: Happy Birthday Trees! programs, respectively. Similar pop-up programs can successfully add engaging hands-on components to any museum's exhibit or programming plans.

STORY TIMES

Working with child audiences offers the unique opportunity to use published stories to tie personal experience to museum collections. Partnering with local libraries provides numerous storybook options that can tie into the museum space. Stories shared in the museum's immersive environment invite listeners to better imagine and experience the tales. Such is the case with the Victoria Mansion's Stories on the Staircase program, as each book is read in a corresponding room of the historic home. These stories can also be paired with an appropriate activity to further comprehension and tie the content to the children's direct experiences. This can be seen with the Children's Museum of Pittsburgh's Maker Story Time as listeners are invited into the museum's makerspace to further explore artistic concepts introduced through the selected story. These storybooks even offer the chance to easily tie museum spaces and collections directly to childhood imaginations and experience, leading this program model to great success, as with the partnered Bookmarks and Landmarks Jr. program at the White River Valley Museum, Neely Mansion, and Mary Olson Farm.

PRESCHOOL TARGETED PROGRAMS

Preschoolers and their adults can be a difficult audience to adequately engage in the museum space. Much of their learning is accomplished through touch and play, activities not often encouraged in museums, but those organizations who set out to actively target this audience can successfully establish the museum as a fun, educational environment. Programs for this group tend to be simpler in scope but no less involved. In fact, they can take the shape of any number of traditional museum programs. For example, the Marietta Museum of History hosts their

Museum Mice Toddler Tour while the Museum of Natural and Cultural History at the University of Oregon uses activity-based learning in their exhibit spaces. Museums are even experimenting with running preschool programs in an otherwise empty museum space. The Shenandoah Valley Discovery Museum opens early for their Itty Bitty Mornings program so participants are able to explore the museum without distraction.

OUTDOOR PROGRAMS

Children often love the outdoors, and taking advantage of this environment can serve many museums well. Utilizing the open space can eliminate many programming concerns, such as group size, space capacity, and even mess in the galleries. In fact, encouraging children to take charge of the outdoor environment can lead to unique interpretive opportunities. The Grand Encampment Museum uses children to manage their summer Pioneer Garden. Children not only plant the garden, but they also weed, water, and harvest it, leading to educational opportunities about biology, pests, and even water conservation.

SOCIAL CLUBS

Children are social, and while they have opportunities to make friends through school, they often seek the chance to gather with other children with like-minded interests. The Kids Klub, hosted by the Daviess County Historical Society Museum, satisfies this need. While each meeting is themed with activities and information, the gatherings focus on peer-to-peer collaboration and discussion rather than interpretive concepts. For the child participants, this is a nice change from other, more formalized youth gatherings.

VOLUNTEER PROGRAMS

Although children are young and inexperienced, they are capable of taking on great responsibility, even within the museum. Finding ways to encourage them to volunteer their time can be mutually beneficial, as they develop skills and knowledge while completing museum tasks otherwise the responsibility of paid staff. The Carbon County Museum utilizes this model with their Youth Tour Ambassadors program. After completing a brief training period, children in the fourth grade and above can spend time assisting professionals with museum duties. Not only does this free the staff from some smaller tasks, but also each volunteer gains crucial knowledge and confidence in the museum field, becoming community ambassadors for the organization.

PROGRAMS FOR CHILDREN AND FAMILIES

Many museums are creating memorable learning experiences for children and their families with little resources. Regardless of mission, topic, or collection, successful programs reach across disciplines to capture children's imaginations. With programs like the Grand Encampment Museum's Pioneer Garden for families and Agecroft Hall's Voyage to Virginia for school groups, museums are capitalizing on their unique stories to reach future audience members.

Voyage to Virginia

Agecroft Hall, Richmond, Virginia
Historic House
School/Partnership
   Target Audience: Grades 3–5
   Attendance: 50–100 students/program
   Overview: In partnership with nearby Henricus Historical Park, Voyage to Virginia walks students through the historic lifestyle of immigrating indentured servants. Through the program, students become indentured servants traveling from England to Virginia. Starting at Agecroft Hall, representing England, students see a slide presentation and tour the historic home to focus on their indentured responsibilities. This includes hands-on activities tied to a student's individual indentured position. The program then continues at Henricus Historical Park, representing historic Virginia, where students run through more interactive tasks and duties, including military drills and even bartering.
   Budget: $0
   Interpretive Components: ★★★★ The immersive nature of this program allows students to interact with the interpretation, and assigning each student a separate indentured identity allows them to explore the concept in more depth.
   Staff Time Requirements: ~12 hours. This program requires a good amount of planning to develop the slide presentation and plan the activities. This is in addition to manning the program.
   Audience Time Requirements: 4.5 hours. The depth of this experience, spanning two different historic sites, requires a significant portion

of time. While the program can be split over two visits, it does require several hours at each location.

Scalability: ★★★ Voyage to Virginia works best with about 60 students, but it can be done with 90. Anything above that number is simply too complicated to manage because of space limitations and staffing availability. Because larger groups require more staff, materials, and coordination, smaller numbers tend to be easier to accommodate.

Analysis: The level of detail associated with this program makes it a challenge to duplicate. Focusing on personalized role–playing requires extensive planning and preparation, and providing contextual background information (done through the slideshow presentation for Voyage to Virginia) is necessary to ground students in the interpretive activities. While many museums would end the program after the presentation, the success of Agecroft Hall's efforts is in the additional time spent acting out the events, situations, and duties associated with the historic roles. Taking the time to extend a school program through role–playing can have extraordinary results, regardless of organizational type.

Healthy Fridays

Shenandoah Valley Discovery Museum, Winchester, Virginia
Children's Museum
Open House/Partnership
   Target Audience: Preschool Children and Families
   Attendance: 50–100 people
   Overview: Every Friday during the college semester, nursing students at nearby Shenandoah University prepare and present health-related activities for pre-K children and their families. This allows students to develop education and presentation skills while offering free interpretive programming for museum visitors. Themes center on health, nutrition, and fitness topics and can range from healthy eating to teeth brushing. These activity stations are available during a two-hour open house held during the museum's regular open hours.
   Budget: $0
   Interpretive Components: ★★★ Audience members rotate through the stations freely, and students are not guaranteed to have experience working with this age group. However, topics can be adapted to include dance, movement, art, and history to expand interpretive exposure.
   Staff Time Requirements: ~3 hours. Museum staff meet preliminarily with a university professor and the nursing students to orient them to the museum and its mission. Further monitoring and assistance are provided as needed during the event. This may include logistical setup, replacing

materials that are running low, or even providing interpretive instruction and assistance to those college students lacking that experience.

Audience Time Requirements: Flexible. Audience members can freely visit each station depending on age, interest, and ability.

Scalability: ★★★★★ The Healthy Fridays model works well with any size audience. At some point, additional stations may need to be added, but the flexibility afforded the audience means any number of people can work through the space during the event.

Analysis: Events like this are heavily dependent on a large, knowledgeable volunteer base willing to dedicate the time and materials. For the Shenandoah Valley Discovery Museum, this is satisfied through the mutually beneficial partnership with the university's nursing school. Participating in Healthy Fridays is required coursework, which ensures continued participation by the nursing students. To duplicate this program, considerable time may be needed to identify and nurture a similar network of partnerships and volunteers. Topics and activity stations can be identified and adjusted based on organizational mission and volunteer skill sets. These discussions should also include who provides activity materials, event space logistics (e.g., tables, cords, etc.), and marketing. Further time may be needed to orient the volunteers to the museum space, mission, goals, and so on and to train them on interacting with the youthful audience.

Hashknife Pony Express Arrival

Western Spirit: Scottsdale's Museum of the West, Scottsdale, Arizona
Art/History Museum
Event/Partnership

    Target Audience: Children and families

    Attendance: More than 200 people

    Overview: In partnership with the Hashknife Pony Express organization, the 250-mile Pony Express mail run is re-created, concluding with delivery at the Western Spirit museum. Audience members can witness the final leg of the mail run, meet the riders and horses, and enjoy multiple–themed activities at the museum. These activities are geared around the history, culture, and influence of the Pony Express and can include demonstrations, discussions, and crafts.

    Budget: $0

    Interpretive Components: ★★★ Information on the Pony Express is provided by event riders and themed activities, and while personal interaction with riders and horses encourages a more meaningful experience, visitors are free to explore the areas that most interest them.

Figure 2.1 Hashknife Pony Express Arrival at the Western Spirit: Scottsdale's Museum of the West

Staff Time Requirement: ~20 hours. Staff time includes planning the event in cooperation with the city of Scottsdale and the Hashknife organization. The event itself requires multiple staff members to manage. This includes crowd control, manning activities, and maintaining the general event space.

Audience Time Requirements: ~1.5 hours. While most audience members arrive for the noon mail drop-off, many stay for the extra events and activities.

Scalability: ★★★★ The event supports several hundred people and is expected to grow. However, smaller audiences must be measured against the amount of staff time required.

Analysis: This event is dependent on the availability of a similar partnering organization and mission-appropriate theme. While the possibility of a similar Pony Express run is recognizably unlikely, museums should be willing to take advantage of other more realistic, though perhaps unconsidered, partnerships. Antique car clubs, hobbyist groups, and even nationally organized events offer great opportunities to provide extensive, immersive programming while expanding the museum's audience reach and advancing its mission objectives. These partnerships will require extensive communication to organize responsibilities and finalize event details, but they can lead to unique and surprising success.

Braille for the Sighted

Museum of the American Printing House for the Blind, Louisville, Kentucky
History Museum
Workshop
   Target Audience: Children age 6 and up
   Attendance: 10–25 people
   Overview: Braille for the Sighted explores Louis Braille and the development of his braille system as a written language. Participants can practice writing on a braille slate and a braillewriter, while older students learn about braille contractions as well as codes for music and math. Information is designed to introduce sighted participants to the complexity and methods of braille and its uses, as well as the history and development of Louis Braille and the written system. Multiple workshops are offered, and participants are free to attend as many as they like.
   Budget: $0
   Interpretive Components: ★★★★ This program allows participants to explore the differences and similarities between braille and the sighted alphabet while working with hands-on opportunities to create their own braille writing, words, music, and even mathematic equations.
   Staff Time Requirements: 2.5 hours. Time includes manning the program, setup, and cleanup.
   Audience Time Requirements: 2 hours. The program runs a full two hours to engage all program components.
   Scalability: ★★ Because of the specialty items required for the hands-on components, smaller groups work much better. Larger groups require more braille slates or writers, which can drive up the budget while decreasing the opportunity for staff–student interactions.
   Analysis: Working with and learning braille can be difficult to fit into an organizational mission, but the concept of codes, alternate languages (both spoken and written), and cryptography are multidisciplinary and can appeal to a variety of museum organizations and audiences. While this program focus requires museum representatives to understand the system well enough to instruct in its use, as well as any necessary crypto machines or tools, it has the potential to engage new audiences in unexpected ways. Interested museums should explore language contexts and variabilities while seeking hands-on opportunities to use and practice the chosen system.

Fourth-Grade Trips

Daviess County Historical Society Museum, Washington, Indiana
History Museum
School

Target Audience: Grade 4
Attendance: 50–100 people
Overview: Instead of traditional tours, local fourth-graders are invited to attend first-person historic reenactments at the Daviess County Historical Society Museum. Museum volunteers portray various historic characters, including Abraham Lincoln, teachers in a one-room school house, and even an Underground Railroader. This not only allows students to interact with history fac-to-face, but it also provides the opportunity to explore personal historic interests through questions and conversations.
Budget: $0
Interpretive Components: ★★★★ Using first-person interpreters encourages students to personally engage with historic figures and time periods. Depending on group size, children are able to converse, ask questions, and interact with the figures, their clothing, and their props.
Staff Time Requirements: ~3 hours. This time includes planning and prep, as well as managing each visit. Initial programming planning may extend this time, as character scripts and performances must be developed, rehearsed, and adjusted depending on group needs.
Audience Time Requirements: 2 hours. Students spend up to two hours learning from and interacting with the characters.
Scalability: ★★★★★ Programs like this can be adapted on a one-on-one basis or performed for large groups, even using a theater stage if necessary. Group size is only limited by program space.
Analysis: While first-person interpretation can be incorporated easily, time to research the character, historic era, and clothing can be time consuming. The interpreter must also be willing to play the part for the necessary time frame. These requirements can make reenactments difficult to perform well, but using staff and volunteers with an interest in acting can greatly improve the quality and success of the programs. Partnerships with local theater groups or even high school drama clubs can provide actors, while museum staff can work to ensure the accuracy and engagement of the scripts, costumes, props, and discussions. Museums can portray any number of characters relative to their mission, including historic figures, scientists, explorers, and even current government representatives.

Credit: The Grace Museum

Figure 2.2 Pop-Up Make N'Take at The Grace Museum

Pop-Up Make N' Take

The Grace Museum, Abilene, Texas
Art/History Museum
Activity-Based
   Target Audience: Children under 10
   Attendance: More than 200 people
   Overview: Every week, free activities are provided in The Grace Museum's children's gallery. These projects are designed for children under 10 years old and encourage hands-on engagement while exploring gallery and exhibit themes. Activities are simple to ensure child accessibility and make use of materials already in stock. They are often tied to current museum exhibits, holidays, or community events to deepen participant understandings and connections. Past activities have included self-portraits, bookmarks, and hand spiders.
   Budget: $0
   Interpretive Components: ★★ Program focus is based on the activity itself, making museum interpretation secondary. However, information linking the activity to museum exhibits can be shared based on interest.

Staff Time Requirements: ~8 hours/week. While activity prep usually takes less than an hour, the activity is manned during open hours once a week.

Audience Time Requirements: ~15 minutes. Audience participants must only commit the time to finish the project, usually about 15 minutes.

Scalability: ★★★★ The Pop-Up Make N' Take program can support small audiences of only a handful of people or large groups that rotate through the space. The only limitation on the program is material and staff availability.

Analysis: The ease of Pop-Up Make N' Take is based largely on its pop-up nature. The program requires very little in the form of setup, uses materials already in stock, and needs minimum staffing to man. This makes it a simple, hassle-free way to engage young audience members with hands-on exploration while providing a handmade object to take home. Similar programs can be adapted for any museum facility regardless of collection or mission as long as materials are available and staff are willing to man the activity.

President's Day Event with Congressman Jim Jordan

Rutherford B. Hayes Presidential Library & Museum, Fremont, Ohio
History Museum/Library
Event/Partnership
  Target Audience: School-age children
  Attendance: 50–100 people

Credit: Rutherford B. Hayes Presidential Library & Museums

Figure 2.3 Congressman Jim Jordan at the President's Day Event at the Rutherford B. Hayes Presidential Library & Museum

Overview: In partnership with Congressman Jim Jordan, the Rutherford B. Hayes Presidential Library & Museum provides questions and
US presidential trivia to schoolchildren and encourages them to research
answers. These questions are then used during an hour-long event where
Congressman Jordan presents these same questions to children for a
chance to win a free horse-drawn sleigh ride through Spiegel Grove, President Hayes's historic estate. The congressman randomly selects which
questions to ask and rotates questions until the child is able to answer
one using their notes.

  Budget: $0

  Interpretive Components: ★★★ All questions are made available to
the children before the event, so they can research their own answers.
Students are even permitted to consult their notes when answering Congressman Jordan's questions.

  Staff Time Requirements: ~20 hours. In addition to general event
setup and cleanup, staff time includes developing and distributing the
questions to area schools as well as coordinating with the congressman's
team.

  Audience Time Requirements: 1 hour. The event runs for one hour,
but participants are free to explore the museum before and after.

  Scalability: ★ The congressman asks at least one question (sometimes
more until a question is answered correctly) to every student participant.
More students mean more time and more space.

  Analysis: This President's Day Event is dependent on the partnership
with an elected official, and many representatives are looking for ways
to interact with constituents. The event can host local, state, and national
representatives or even a combination of the three. Museums willing to
invest the time and energy to develop and nurture such a relationship
can leverage it for a similar program. Time must also be spent developing
and distributing the mission- or event-oriented trivia questions, as well as
securing appropriate prizes.

Start with Art

Mabee-Gerrer Museum of Art, Shawnee, Oklahoma
Art/History Museum
School

  Target Audience: Early childhood through grade 12

  Attendance: 50–100 people

  Overview: The Start with Art program uses gallery exhibited artworks
as a springboard to explore such multidisciplinary subjects as language
arts, science, math, and social studies. The program includes a guided
tour, corresponding art activity, and student-centered discussions in a

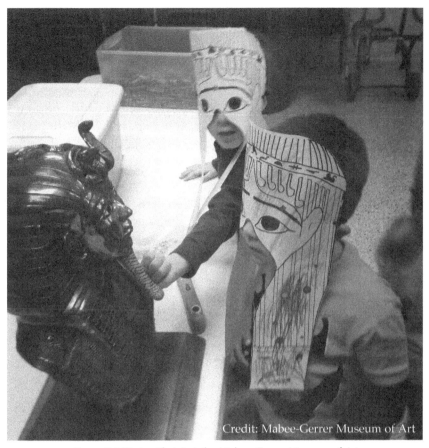

Credit: Mabee-Gerrer Museum of Art

Figure 2.4 Start with Art at the Mabee-Gerrer Museum of Art

teacher-chosen focus area. Focus areas include ancient Egypt, ancient Greece, medieval Europe, and sub-Saharan Africa. Plans for a Native American focus are in development.

Budget: $1/student

Interpretive Components: ★★★★ Using Visual Thinking Strategies (VTS), students are guided through the chosen focus area by trained staff, as conversations concentrate on historic, cultural, and technical interpretation as portrayed through selected objects and student-centered discussions. Discussed concepts are then applied in a corresponding art activity.

Staff Time Requirements: ~45 hours. Each focus area must be planned for concept development, focus object selection, and art activity. This can take between 20 and 40 hours. One docent is needed for every 20 students to complete scheduling, setup, facilitation, and cleanup. The program itself requires about three and a half hours per docent. Additional docent training in using vVisual Thinking Strategies may be needed to properly facilitate each program.

Audience Time Requirements: 2 hours. Teachers must commit to two hours at the museum to complete each program.

Scalability: ★★★ Start with Art can be scaled smaller by simply addressing the amount of materials needed. The more students, the more staff are required. Programs with 75 students require 4 facilitators and an extra staff member to handle rotations. Programs with as many as 125 students can be managed by adding additional time, staff, and activities.

Analysis: Start with Art uses Visual Thinking Strategies to encourage deeper critical thinking by tying art to other disciplines. The VTS method uses open-ended, observational questions about art to draw students into conversations about history, science, math, and language arts. These discussions are then paired with corresponding activities to further increase comprehension. While the high staff time required to learn how to utilize VTS and to develop this program creates some challenges in replicating Start with Art, similar programs using VTS with art and historic objects can successfully replace traditional school tour formats.

Stories on the Staircase

Victoria Mansion, Portland, Maine
Historic House
In-Gallery/Partnership/Story Time
   Target Audience: Preschool children
   Attendance: 10–25 people
   Overview: During the holiday season, the Victoria Mansion pairs storybooks from the local library with specifically decorated rooms in their historic house to immerse preschool children in historic stories and themes. Each week, two stories are read, followed by a visit to a room that corresponds to the characters and plot of the chosen books. Museum staff explore these spaces with the children by literally seeing it on their level; staff often present the program on their knees to be face-to-face with the audience while interacting with the historic room from their perspective. Participants are sent home with suggested complimentary activity instructions.
   Budget: $10/year
   Interpretive Components: ★★★★ The program allows museum staff to concentrate on content and themes designed for the preschool audience. Chosen themes and story elements help to draw the young audience into the historic space and grow their appreciation for it.

Figure 2.5 Victoria Mansion Staircase for Stories on the Staircase

Staff Time Requirements: 8 hours. Staff require about four hours to plan the event. This includes selecting the storybooks, developing connections to the historic house, and choosing corresponding activities. The roughly one-hour event requires three museum representatives to adequately engage the audience.

Audience Time Requirements: ~1 hour. Stories on the Staircase runs roughly an hour to read two stories and explore two separate spaces.

Scalability: ★★★ This event can be scaled depending on space and staff availability. Smaller groups work better with smaller spaces and staff limitations, but larger groups can be accommodated using space rotations and larger staffs.

Analysis: Story times are great ways to engage the preschool audience while connecting them to historic spaces and exhibits. Because a high number of staff is needed (about 3 staff for every 15 audience members), both to encourage audience engagement and to protect the collection from little fingers, replicability of this event is based largely on the number of staff available. While similar events could simply involve reading a story in the museum space, taking additional time to explore a display corresponding to the book further connects preschool experiences to the museum, making it a welcoming and fun space.

Special Nights for Special Needs

Children's Museum of Richmond, Richmond, Virginia
Children's Museum
Open House

Target Audience: Children and families with special needs

Attendance: 10–25 people

Overview: Special Nights for Special Needs is a monthly recurring open house where the museum space is adapted to accommodate the unique needs of children and families with special needs. Museum staff facilitate adapted activities and specialized play areas for participants to enjoy the museum in an environment that boasts a smaller number of visitors, intentionally designed low-sensory activities, and designated cool-down spaces.

Budget: $10/event

Interpretive Components: ★★★ These Special Nights may simply open museum spaces for use, or they may be themed to highlight certain exhibits or activities. Having most staff available allows a high staff-to-participant ratio to ensure engagement and audience comfort.

Staff Time Requirements: ~20 hours/month. Event planning, manning the event, and cleaning up constitute staff time requirements. If staff are unfamiliar with this audience's special requirements, additional training may be required.

Audience Time Requirements: Flexible. The event runs for two hours, and participants have the flexibility to stay as long as they desire.

Scalability: ★★★★★ This program is very simple to scale, as attendance does not affect costs. The only limitations are those placed by space

Credit: Children's Museum of Richmond

Figure 2.6 Bruce and George at Special Nights for Special Needs at the Children's Museum of Richmond

logistics and by trained staff to maintain a desirable staff-to-participant ratio.

Analysis: The open-house nature of the event makes it fairly easy to replicate. Duplicating this event requires the willingness to open the museum during nonregular hours and gauging the amount of prior experience current staff have with the special-needs community. These needs are varied and require flexibility, gentleness, and creative solutions. Without staff committed to working with this audience or at least showing the willingness to train if no prior experience exists, this program model can be a challenge.

Preschool Story Time

History Colorado Center, Denver, Colorado
History Museum
In-Gallery/Partnership/Story Time
   Target Audience: Preschool children and families
   Attendance: 25–50 people
   Overview: Every month, staff open the museum early to host story times in galleries. Early open times allow young learners to explore these spaces with their caregivers without the regular museum crowd.

Figure 2.7 Preschool Story Time at the History Colorado Center

All books come from the Denver Public Library and are accompanied by staff-made flannel boards to further connect the space with the story.

Budget: $15

Interpretive Components: ★★★★ Connecting exhibit themes to the story through the visual flannel boards, songs, and rhymes exposes the young audience to the museum and gallery spaces in engaging and personal ways.

Staff Time Requirements: ~1–2 hours. Planning time includes selecting the story, identifying associated songs and rhymes, creating the flannel storyboards, and connecting these pieces to an existing gallery exhibit.

Audience Time Requirements: 30 minutes. The planned story time takes approximately 30 minutes with the opportunity to explore the rest of the museum once galleries (those unused by the program) open.

Scalability: ★★★★★ The Preschool Story Time easily accommodates larger groups and can be scaled smaller depending on the gallery space available.

Analysis: A gallery-centered story time can be comfortably duplicated depending on gallery space and available themes. The History Colorado Center's Preschool Story Time goes a step farther and includes visual storytelling elements beyond the book illustrations and exhibit displays through the flannel storyboards. Additional interactive components, such as rhymes and movement, help to deepen these connections. These simple yet effective efforts incorporate multiple senses and play into learning, a vital component of preschool comprehension.

Fall History Day

Cass County Historical Society, West Fargo, North Dakota
History Museum
Event/Open House
   Target Audience: Homeschool children and families
   Attendance: More than 200 people
   Overview: The annual Fall History Day is designed for homeschool families to explore history in a fun and hands-on environment. Volunteers demonstrate historic crafts and processes and invite attendees to participate. Activity stations include washing and spinning wool, one-room schoolhouse lessons, blacksmith forges, Native American bison use, and packing activities for Norwegian immigrants (circa 1900).
   Budget: $20
   Interpretive Components: ★★★★★ Audience members are open to many interpretive opportunities based on their interests and time availability. The variety of activities means the audience can experience as many topics in as much depth as they want.
   Staff Time Requirements: ~40 hours. Staff time can be significant, as event logistics, volunteer coordination, event setup, and event cleanup are required. While most volunteers willingly provide their own materials, some additional supplies may need to be purchased. Staff must also provide any necessary volunteer training to equip docents to man their activities.
   Audience Time Requirements: Flexible. Homeschool families have the flexibility to stay for as long as they like, depending on their interests, time commitments, and educational needs.
   Scalability: ★★★★ This event is very demanding on the front end, but it can accommodate up to several hundred people, depending on space. The event has the potential to reach beyond the initial expected number as long as there is enough volunteer commitment and space availability.
   Analysis: Fall History Day is targeted specifically to the local home-school community. This audience often has differing educational goals and expectations for their visit, which can be met through the variety of stations offered. These stations are only possible through extensive volunteer commitments. If a dedicated volunteer base is not readily available, museums can develop such a network by specifically inviting individuals and organizations associated with the chosen theme. For Fall History Day, these include historic crafts associated with Norwegian immigration. Other organizations can alter these themes based on mission and volunteer availability. Spatial needs are dependent on the size of the local homeschool population. While spaces able to accommodate large groups of people participating at various activity stations are often not available

on museum grounds, time may need to be spent to find them. This can further complicate event planning, but it can lead to further extending the program's reach and audience availability.

Maker Story Time

Children's Museum of Pittsburgh, Pittsburgh, Pennsylvania
Children's Museum
In-Gallery/Partnership/Story Time
   Target Audience: Children and families
   Attendance: Less than 10 people per program
   Overview: The Maker Story Time is paired with a professional maker-space to encourage children to explore a variety of components involved in the creative process. Participants are invited to listen to and participate in the story time. Books are chosen based on a selected theme tied to the creative process, such as materials, methods, or artistic styles. Accompanying activities in the makerspace, using professional tools and materials, reinforce these themes.
   Budget: $20
   Interpretive Components: ★★★★ Books and activities can support any visual, design, or creative theme to explore the process and components of artistic creation.
   Staff Time Requirements: ~1.5 hours/program. Staff must select themes, books, and activities in addition to facilitating the approximately hour-long program.
   Audience Time Requirements: ~1 hour. Participants can choose to simply listen to the story, or they can stay longer to take part in the activity. Most stay for about an hour.
   Scalability: ★★ This program works best with audiences of 10 or fewer. Larger groups are more difficult to engage in the paired activity and to manage in the highly active makerspace.
   Analysis: The Maker Story Time uses an adult-oriented professional makerspace to instruct children in the processes, tools, and methods of artistic expression. Themed tie-ins between the book and access to the professional tools and materials allows participants to expand their personal understandings and experiences using relative stories and "real" adult spaces. While it is understood that most museums do not have access to a makerspace, offering a combined story and activity time tied to professional jobs, tools, and themes is possible across most museum types and resources. The key is not to dumb down or cater to the audience's age but instead to incorporate specialized skills and methods in a comprehensive yet relatable environment.

Museum Mice Toddler Tour

Marietta Museum of History, Marietta, Georgia
History Museum
Tour

    Target Audience: Preschool children and parents

    Attendance: 10–25 people/tour

    Overview: Every month, the Museum Mice Toddler Tour uses mice mascots to introduce toddlers to historic themes and topics. Using basic concepts, like shapes, sounds, games, jobs, and so on, each tour is themed to offer a variety of activities, stories, and crafts using museum exhibits and objects.

    Budget: $20

    Interpretive Components: ★★★★★ Tours are themed to focus on a simple concept, introduced through a specific gallery exhibit space. Different themes allow for different galleries to be explored. Tour concepts are specifically designed for preschool audiences for retention and engagement. This includes the use of movement, color, repetition, and rhyming schemes.

    Staff Time Requirements: 1–4 hours. Staff must design and test the tour activities, and to maintain a small child-to-adult ratio, two staff members may be needed for each tour.

    Audience Time Requirements: 45 minutes. Tours run about 45 minutes, and there are no preparation or postvisit requirements

    Scalability: ★★ The Museum Mice Toddler Tour works best with smaller groups to ensure adequate supervision and to encourage engagement. The more children for the program, the more staff are required, with potentially multiple tours (meaning multiple staff) necessary.

    Analysis: Taking preschool children on an organized museum tour can be difficult. Short attention spans, needed movement, and limited cognitive complexity make this program model a challenge. However, the Museum Mice Toddler Tour overcomes these issues by focusing on very specific themes as they appear throughout exhibit galleries. This increases movement, focuses attention, and broadens experiences as groups move through the museum space. These themes are further targeted by using a mascot or animal representative to help direct information. Other organizations willing to develop this focused approach with this young audience can see similar success. Finding similar colors, shapes, animals, emotions, and other themes helps tie galleries together in a cohesive and fun tour designed to make the museum a fun and educational environment welcoming to preschoolers and their families.

Neighborhoods

Johnson County Jim Gatchell Memorial Museum, Buffalo, Wyoming
History Museum
School

Target Audience: Grade 2

Attendance: 50–100 people

Overview: Neighborhoods is a two-part program codesigned with teachers to meet state education standards. The first part of the program explores the types, purposes, and community components of public art, while the second part uses contemporary and historic community photos for students to match to specific locations. Each student orally shares their findings and defends their decisions and correlations with classmates.

Budget: $20

Interpretive Components: ★★★★ The program explores public art as it ties to community cultures, as well as explores how places change over time. This sparks the discussion of local and national history. Students must use critical thinking exercises and presentation skills to defend their decisions to the group.

Staff Time Requirements: ~40 hours. Planning time can take up to 35 hours to find public art examples, create the presentation, curate collec-

Credit: Johnson County Jim Gatchell Memorial Museum

Figure 2.8 Neighborhoods school program at the Johnson County Jim Gatchell Memorial Museum

tion photographs, and collect contemporary community photographs for the program. The total program takes about an hour and is used several times a year.

Audience Time Requirements: 1 hour. It takes about an hour to cover both programming sections. This can be done in a single meeting or split among multiple visits.

Scalability: ★★★★★ This program is already designed to handle a large number of participants, as photos are split among small break-out groups. Each program component can be used as independent programs to further adjust for time and audience size. Smaller groups can even be given more time for certain program components.

Analysis: The Neighborhoods program has a high time component on the front end but is low maintenance once established. It also largely depends on the amount of public art and historic photographs that are available for a community. Museums interested in exploring similar community-themed programs should be willing to take the time to match local themes to state educational standards, making the program useful in meeting teachers' educational goals. These standards can be found on state education departmental websites. Utilizing public art, local historic sites, small business development, and so on offers opportunities for multidisciplinary exploration and hands-on activities that encourage the development of critical thinking and 21st-Century Skills. Both further drive the importance and validity of the program for local curriculums.

Pioneer Garden

Grand Encampment Museum, Encampment, Wyoming
History Museum
Community Exhibit
   Target Audience: Local community children
   Attendance: 10–25 people
   Overview: The outdoor Pioneer Garden is planted, maintained, and harvested by community children. Staff use the garden space to teach the importance and scope of work that historic gardens presented to western settlers, and children volunteer to visit the garden two to three times a week to water, weed, and care for the crops. The program starts in early spring as museum staff and community children come together to prepare the garden space and plant the selected crops. Visits continue throughout the summer to maintain the space, and children gather with staff again in the fall to harvest and close the garden.
   Budget: $25
   Interpretive Components: ★★★★★ The garden offers multiple avenues for interpretation, including planting, environmental impacts, water

Credit: Grand Encampment Museum

Figure 2.9 Gardeners work at the Pioneer Garden at the Grand Encampment Museum

conservation, effects of insects and rodents, use of garden tools, and more. All interpretive opportunities are offered through direct, hands-on experience.

Staff Time Requirements: ~40 hours. Staff time includes garden prep, supervising the children, caring for the garden, and helping with the harvest.

Audience Time Requirements: ~7 hours. In addition to the 2-hour initial planting event, children return for 30 minutes each week for 8 to 12 weeks to continue garden maintenance. The museum's location within a small community makes it easy for participants to walk to the garden at their convenience.

Scalability: ★★★ The size of the garden is directly related to the size of the volunteer audience, as well as the space and materials available. Larger gardens require a larger volunteer force and vice versa. This also affects the amount of seeds, tools, water, work, and so on as needed.

Analysis: Teaching gardening and food cultivation can be an enlightening childhood experience, and using an actual garden deepens concept comprehension. Giving participants the responsibility and ownership for maintaining a garden allows them to benefit from the experience, both in terms of eating the garden's produce and applying classroom subjects (e.g., biology, water cycles, environments, etc.) through sustaining the plants. Expanding the garden concept to focus on pioneer techniques and plant selection allows a multidisciplinary approach, as history and technological advancements are included. Museums seeking similar projects must have access to the appropriate garden space—whether on the museum grounds or through a community garden area—and be willing to instruct and supervise participants throughout the process. This can require significant dedication and commitment, especially for off-site garden plots.

Kids Klub

Daviess County Historical Society Museum, Washington, Indiana
History Museum
Social Club

Target Audience: Kindergarten through grade 5 students and caregivers
Attendance: 10–25 people
Overview: Kids Klub is a free, regularly scheduled program for children to gather socially with their adults. Each meeting is themed with related stories and activities, and they even include surprise presenters and snacks. Klub gatherings occur one Saturday each month and are designed to encourage peer-to-peer and child-to-caregiver exploration and discovery. Topics are themed to coordinate with Daviess County history and events, inspiring deeper connections and personal correlations.
Budget: $25

Interpretive Components: ★★★★ Kids Klub allows children to explore historic themes in an easy, social setting through engaging activities. Participants are encouraged to learn through stories, interactives, and collaboration with their peers and their adults.

Staff Time Requirements: 12 hours. The program requires about four hours of planning and preparation to develop themes and corresponding activities. Each meeting needs about four staff members to facilitate meeting components.

Audience Time Requirements: 2 hours. Each meeting takes two hours to include all program activities.

Scalability: ★★★ This program works best with smaller participant groups to create a more comfortable environment for socializing and peer-to-peer cooperation.

Analysis: Managing a children's social group takes planning and dedication. Activities must be age appropriate, satisfy mission-oriented goals, encourage social collaboration, and urge self-discovery. Further staff commitment must be nurtured to develop these activities and then step back to allow Klub members to work together to complete projects instead of direct staff intervention. Museums willing to take the time to develop similar meetings can expand themes and topics to include science, history, and art through books, guest visitors, museum objects, and hands-on activities.

Artifact Detective and Exhibit Label Workshop

Historical Museum at Fort Missoula, Missoula, Montana
Historic Site/History Museum
School/Workshop

Target Audience: Local school students

Attendance: 25–50 people

Overview: The Artifact Detective and Exhibit Label Workshop uses museum education collections to introduce students to critically thinking about objects and their role in personal historic narratives. Participants are led through basic exhibit development as they learn how to handle museum objects; ask open, descriptive questions; and write an exhibit label. Final labels are then compared with curator-written labels.

Budget: $50

Interpretive Components: ★★★ This program teaches critical thinking skills and explores historic time periods through individual objects. Object categorization is also explored by comparing different objects among the class groups.

Staff Time Requirements: ~9 hours. The program requires up to five hours to theme the content, plan the class discussion, and select the

Figure 2.10 Artifact Detective and Exhibit Label Workshop at the Historical Museum at Fort Missoula

objects. Manning the program can take up to three hours, with an additional hour for cleanup.

Audience Time Requirements: ~1.5 hours. The program is flexible, depending on how much time the teacher schedules. Discussions and interpretive writing instructions can be incredibly detailed or very brief. Some teachers have even requested multiple meetings to explore different aspects of the program, requiring up to a total of three hours to complete.

Scalability: ★★★★ The number of students who can participate depends on the number of available objects. The program can be done with as few as four students but can accommodate many more. However, more students require more objects. Even having participants working in teams can only accommodate four to five people per group.

Analysis: The Artifact Detective and Exhibit Label Workshop introduces school-age children to the workings of a museum and the process of researching and displaying objects to tell a specific story. As such, museums simply require staff time and an available teaching or education collection to produce the program. However, programmatic success depends on staff's ability to facilitate student inquiry and communication skills to tie objects to historic narratives and then to clearly communicate these ties through written labels. This is rarely accomplished through brief discussions and often requires detailed coaching and open staff–student interactions.

Children's Battle of Lexington Reenactment

Lexington Historical Society, Lexington, Massachusetts
History Museum/Historic Site
School
 Target Audience: Children
 Attendance: 50–100

*Figure 2.11 Children's Battle of Lexington Reenactment
at the Lexington Historical Society*

Overview: To explore the Battle of Lexington, children train with reenactors to be military soldiers. Groups representing both the American militia and British regulars learn about the daily lives and responsibilities of the soldiers as well as the specifics of the Battle of Lexington. After the training period, students march to the Lexington Battle Green and reenact the historic engagement.

Budget: $50

Interpretive Components: ★★★★ Children actively engage with reenactors and staff to learn the details of both the historic battle and the soldiers' daily lives. The hands-on interpretation combines history with play to explore battle history and site details.

Staff Time Requirements: ~6 hours/staff member. Staff time includes registration and running the event. The number of reenactors required depends on the number of children involved. Roughly 1 reenactor can work with each group of 12 to 15 students.

Audience Time Requirements: 1.5 hours. Each reenactment runs one and a half hours. This includes the training and interpretive components, as well as the final battle reenactment.

Scalability: ★★★ Because the program takes place outside, the size of the group can be easily accommodated, given that there are enough reenactors and staff available. Larger groups allow for a more involved reenactment. Smaller groups are more difficult to direct in re-creating the battle.

Analysis: While a children's battle reenactment program is notably specific to site and mission, encouraging children to learn and re-create historic events can be incorporated into any historic museum mission. This model combines learning and play, as it requires program participants to internalize interpretive information in order to creatively solve historic problems and situations their characters face. Large group reenactments require participant collaboration and cooperation in addition to understanding selected historic roles. To see similar success, staff should be willing to establish historical context, walk participants through role details, and then encourage first-person character reenactments.

Summer STEAM: Signal Flags and Semaphore

US Naval Undersea Museum, Keyport, Washington
Science/History Museum
In-Gallery
  Target Audience: Children
  Attendance: 50–100 people

Credit: US Naval Undersea Museum

Figure 2.12 Summer STEAM: Signal Flags and Semaphore at the United States Naval Undersea Museum

Overview: Over the summer, the US Naval Undersea Museum hosts 10 different STEAM programs themed to include science, technology, engineering, art, and mathematic concepts focused on maritime and oceanic topics. The Signal Flags and Semaphore program focuses on the importance of visual communication to the US Navy. Participants learn several visual signals, create their own signal flag messages, and communicate through semaphore.

Budget: $50

Interpretive Components: ★★★ This program provides information in several areas, including visual languages, international communications, and history. However, because the audience can leave at any time, the amount of time (and information) dedicated to interpretation varies.

Staff Time Requirements: ~12 hours. The program requires at least one staff person over the four-hour course, in addition to development, setup, and cleanup.

Audience Time Requirements: Flexible. While the program is available for a four-hour rotation, audience participants have the flexibility to decide how long and how involved they get.

Scalability: ★★★★★ This program requires very little in terms of materials and staff and could be easily scaled larger or smaller, depending on the space and materials available.

Analysis: The US Naval Undersea Museum utilizes the STEAM approach for their themed summer activities. STEAM is an educational method that represents a combined science, technology, engineering, art, and mathematics disciplinary focus. Each programming option must include at least two of these fields to encourage cross-curricula under-standings and applications while tying topics to the museum's program-ming goals. Selected interpretation and activities must both include one of the recognized disciplines and meet the organization's mission. This focus helps determine summer STEAM programs and connects chosen themes to classroom lessons. Other museums interested in advancing a similar STEAM approach must be willing to explore art's influence on mathematics and engineering and technology's connection to science and vice versa through audience-centered activities and interpretation.

Youth Tour Ambassadors

Carbon County Museum, Rawlins, Wyoming
History Museum
Volunteer
    Target Audience: Local children and youth
    Attendance: Less than 10 people

Overview: Starting in the fourth grade, four local students are eligible to participate in Carbon County Museum's summer Youth Tour Ambas-sadors program. Participants receive customer service training and basic

Credit: Lauren E. Hunley

Figure 2.13 2016 Youth Tour Ambassadors at Carbon County Museum

collections-handling instruction to help staff with museum operations. Each student is required to volunteer approximately 25 hours over the summer. Their responsibilities include researching and installing a temporary exhibit, managing visitor sign-in, and planning and executing their own open-house event.

Budget: $50

Interpretive Components: ★★★★ Ambassadors are introduced to museum operations, customer service practices, and research and exhibit methods. Other training and interpretation occurs on an individual basis, depending on need and interest.

Staff Time Requirements: ~82 hours. Most staff time is spent managing volunteers during their shifts. Some additional time for planning and marketing is also included.

Audience Time Requirements: ~30 hours. Program participants are required to volunteer at least 25 hours over the summer. Additional time is needed to plan and host the Ambassador Open House at the program's conclusion.

Scalability: ★ This program requires a low volunteer–staff ratio to ensure understanding and participant and collections safety. Additional volunteers would require additional staff time (approximately 20 hours per volunteer) and the availability of appropriate tasks.

Analysis: Bringing children into the museum as volunteers establishes a museum-friendly foundation for them as they grow. Becoming familiar with museum operations, departmental duties, and customer service needs develops professional skills at an early age. Learning research methods and interacting with peers and museum staff in a professional environment illustrates how responsibility for specific museum tasks can grow critical thinking skills and build confidence. Further, involving youth in museum operations invites family and friends to take an interest in their duties and, by association, in the museum. Although managing a program with such young volunteers requires significant commitment, museums willing to dedicate the time to training and managing youth volunteers can help solidify their involvement and commitment to the museum and its future projects.

Darwin Day

Kenosha Public Museum, Kenosha, Wisconsin
Science/Art Museum
Open House
  Target Audience: Children and families
  Attendance: More than 200 people

Overview: Designed to celebrate the life and work of Charles Darwin, the Dinosaur Discovery Museum in the Kenosha Public Museum uses hands-on activities, games, crafts, and talks by local college professors to help visitors learn about Darwin, the theory of evolution, and natural selection. The open house allows visitors to wander through selected activities; see visiting wildlife, such as turtles, pythons, and frogs; and take part in field-specific discussions covering biology, paleontology, and other evolutionary-related areas.

Budget: $50

Interpretive Components: ★★★★ The program not only introduces Darwin and the concepts of evolution and natural selection to a young audience, but it also provides the opportunity to address common misconceptions about the theories and concepts surrounding evolution.

Staff Time Requirements: ~18 hours. Time includes planning the event, coordinating the outside speakers, setup, and managing the event with several staff members.

Audience Time Requirements: Flexible. The flexibility of the event allows audience members to explore at their own pace. Families may spend five minutes listening to a speaker, or they may spend an hour exploring different activity options.

Scalability: ★★★★ This event can handle as many people as the space allows.

Analysis: The Darwin Day celebration uses a single person's lifework to theme the event. This provides the opportunity to unite multiple fields, activities, and discussions while structuring the interpretation to appeal to a younger audience. Exploring the multiple faces of this unifying theme ensures visitors the chance to find their interests and relative perspectives, drawing them into deeper comprehension. While finding comparable artists, scientists, or other key figures to theme similar events may seem straightforward, evaluating disciplines, themes, and corresponding activities requires detailed attention and can take up considerable time. This, in addition to planning and managing the event, involves a dedicated event staff for an audience not guaranteed to experience all program components.

Summer Pop-Up

Cape Fear Museum, Wilmington, North Carolina
History/Science Museum
In-Gallery
   Target Audience: Children and families
   Attendance: 10–25 people

Overview: Over the summer, the Cape Fear Museum offers drop-in activities in their galleries. Designed to encourage discovery and hands-on learning, children explore themed crafts and experiments with their adults. Programs are activity based and designed for short time commitments. They have included working with electric circuits, furs and skulls, movies and film, and the indigenous people of the Cape Fear area.

Budget: $50

Interpretive Components: ★★★ The pop-up programs are designed to foster discovery and experiments versus instruction-based learning. Any brief interpretation is used to guide participants through these activities.

Staff Time Requirements: 1 hour/program. Staff time per program is minimal, but multiple programs are often scheduled a day.

Audience Time Requirements: ~20 minutes. Participants are free to explore as their interests permit, but completing all components of a themed activity usually takes about a half-hour.

Scalability: ★★★★ Over the course of the pop-up, program activities can support as many participants as space and materials allow.

Analysis: Introducing brief, activity-based learning activities requires very little in relation to space and materials. Even staff time is reduced to basic interpretation and hands-on instruction. Participatory learning encourages self-discovery, family collaboration, and creative problem solving. Selected experiments and crafts can inspire greater curiosity and deeper understandings without needed extensive budget or staff commitments. Even space is flexible, as program components can occur in exhibit, classroom, or outdoor spaces. Providing similar in-gallery activity programming can be adapted by any museum willing to provide the necessary elements.

Little Wonders

UO Museum of Natural and Cultural History, Eugene, Oregon
Science/History Museum
In-Gallery

Target Audience: Preschool children and families

Attendance: 25–50 people

Overview: Every month, museum staff host preschool-age-appropriate activities in the museum's galleries. Activities combine learning and play with appropriate interactives, including crafts, stories, songs, games, dress-up, and exhibit exploration. Each month is themed with changing corresponding activities to investigate topics on an early-education level. Science discussions center on curiosity and experimentation. Carnivores are discovered through gallery scavenger hunts and crafts. All program components encourage self-discovery through play to target this pre-school audience.

Budget: $50/month

Interpretive Components: ★★★ All activities are themed to match gallery exhibits. The level of staff interpretation depends on audience size and the complexity of the activity.

Staff Time Requirements: ~6 hours. Staff time includes planning, setup, program management, and cleanup.

Audience Time Requirements: 1 hour. Themed activities are designed to take an hour, but participants are free to continue exploring the museum before and after the scheduled program.

Scalability: ★★ Little Wonders works best with smaller audiences to ensure engagement. The ability to accommodate larger audiences depends on the type and complexity of the scheduled activities. Larger groups also require increased space and materials.

Analysis: Including preschoolers in museum programming may seem intimidating or even unnecessary, but drawing this audience into the museum helps make gallery spaces fun, educational, and playful for both young audiences and their accompanying adults. Little Wonders invites this audience on a recurring basis by alternating themes, activities, and exhibit locations, encouraging repeat visits based on interest and learning opportunities. While the recurring nature of this program requires a higher staff time commitment in planning and management, the continued successful interaction between preschoolers and museum themes provides a worthy return.

Bookmarks and Landmarks Jr.

White River Valley Museum, Neely Mansion, and Mary Olson Farm, Auburn, Washington
History Museum/Historic Site
Story Time/Partnership

Target Audience: Children and families

Attendance: 25–50 people

Overview: Bookmarks and Landmarks Jr. is a partnership between the King County Library System and three local historic sites. Librarians choose books that relate to the history and mission of each site. These stories are then read at the corresponding site, where special tours, activities, and guided book discussions take place. Using selected books as inspiration, these special activities often explore themes, events, and locations covered in the story. Discussions allow more detailed interpretation and encourage historic connections with personal experience. These can be led by librarians, museum staff, and even the occasional author.

Budget: $60

Interpretive Components: ★★★★ This partnership allows audience members to enjoy each site through story as they are given opportunities to complete duties, taste foods, and handle objects described in the book. The accompanying discussion explores audience feelings, opinions, and relative experiences that relate back to the story's main characters.

Staff Time Requirements: ~15 hours/site. The program requires multiple meetings and consistent communication between the partnering organizations. This is in addition to developing the site-specific activities, facilitating program components, and cleanup.

Audience Time Requirements: 1.5 hours. The program runs about one and a half hours per site to complete all components.

Scalability: ★★ This program depends heavily on the audience's ability to participate in site activities and to discuss their discoveries during the guided conversation. This is most easily attained through small group audiences, as larger groups greatly detract from this ability.

Analysis: Bookmarks and Landmarks Jr. combines two successful programming models—story times and in-gallery activities—to create a blended program that explores historic site themes through several guided, interpretive activities. Using stories to draw audiences into the space and then introducing corresponding objects, foods, and crafts tangibly and emotionally connect participants to the space and its associated history. Accompanying discussions further solidify these connections by allowing audience members to explore the reactions and associations generated by their experience. This program even encourages repeat visitors by rotating site locations and their associated stories and activities. Similar museum–library partnerships (with activities and discussion) could be possible for any organization, regardless of mission or location.

Sewing and Circuits

Cape Fear Museum, Wilmington, North Carolina
History/Science/Culture Museum
Workshop

Target Audience: Children age 8 to 12 with accompanying adult

Attendance: 10–25 people

Overview: Using sewing and crafting materials, participants explore circuitry by making wearable, light-up felt pins using LED lights. Participants use a multidisciplinary approach to explore electricity, sewing, and creative thinking, as each craft incorporates conductive thread and LEDs to create unique, DIY pins.

Budget: $75

Credit: Cape Fear Museum

Figure 2.14 Sewing and Circuits at the Cape Fear Museum

Interpretive Components: ★★★ To successfully create the pin, participants must understand basic sewing techniques and parallel circuitry. Both topics are covered by hands-on instruction through the workshop.

Staff Time Requirements: ~6 hours. Each workshop requires one staff member for every four to five participants. This means most groups require multiple staff.

Audience Time Requirements: 1.5 hours. Each workshop runs about an hour and a half to complete the LED light-up pin. This includes basic sewing instruction, circuit explanations, and creating the pin.

Scalability: ★★★ As mentioned, larger groups require additional staff familiar with the project, as well as more materials. Smaller staff availability necessitates smaller groups, regardless of material and space.

Analysis: Sewing and Circuits combines two seemingly unrelated activities to create unique, imaginative accessories participants can take home. It breaks down supposed gender expectations and blends science, engineering, art, and life skills in a fun, hands-on environment. This requires students to use creative problem-solving skills and experimentation while fostering artistic creativity and new skill development. Although prior knowledge of both circuitry and sewing is required to successfully duplicate this program, the options for combined disciplines are nearly endless. Crochet and construction can be paired to teach wildlife studies, water tides, food science, and needlework through building a netted fish trap. Automobiles can be combined with cooking to teach mechanical engineering, chemistry, food science, auto mechanics, and filtration by exploring the creation and use of biofuels. Similar multidisciplinary programs can be developed based on staff knowledge and familiarity.

Canning Creations

Friends of the Pound House Foundation, Dripping Springs, Texas
Historic Site
Workshop
   Target Audience: Children and families
   Attendance: 25–50 people
   Overview: Using cucumbers and dill from the historic site's garden, Canning Creations leads children through the process of canning and food preservation, from garden to table. Participants are guided through canning methods, including food prep, sterilization, seasoning, and packing and sealing the jars to create take-home pickles. They even have the opportunity to decorate their jars using fabric, ribbon, and other craft materials.
   Budget: $75
   Interpretive Components: ★★★★ As the process of canning includes discussions on chemistry and botany, participants are exposed to multiple interpretive topics. This interpretation also contains information on the historic home and garden site.
   Staff Time Requirements: ~6 hours. This time includes prepping materials and manning the event. It does not include managing the garden harvest.
   Audience Time Requirements: 2 hours. To follow the entire process from harvest to sealed preserves, each canning workshop runs about two hours.
   Scalability: ★★★ Because of the complexity of the canning process, the Canning Creations workshop works best with smaller groups to allow everyone equal hands-on opportunities. Groups of more than 30 would require significant additions to staff and materials.
   Analysis: The practice of traditional crafts and lifeways, like food preservation, has seen a noticeable resurgence in recent years. Museums are in a unique position to share these processes and instruct in their application. Extending these programming models to include children allows museums to explore numerous discussions on history, science, engineering, biology, life science, mathematics, and even art in a single workshop.

Credit: Friends of the Pound House Foundation

Figure 2.15 Canning Creations with the Friends of the Pound House Foundation

In addition, the workshop exposes youth to the complexity and practice of these crafts while connecting this information to their personal experience. Classes focusing on traditional crafts can be based on those subjects staff know, or they can invite guest instructors to share their knowledge.

Itty Bitty Mornings

Shenandoah Valley Discovery Museum, Winchester, Virginia
Children's Museum
In-Gallery/Open House
   Target Audience: Preschool children and families
   Attendance: 25–50 people
   Overview: Twice a month, the Discovery Museum is opened early to toddlers and their adults with special themed activities focusing on developing communication skills, processing, patience, and fine motor skills. Activity stations include sensory bins, science experiments, animal exploration, music, and sign language. Audience members are encouraged to explore the museum without large crowds and school groups.
   Budget: $75
   Interpretive Components: ★★★ Activities are specially designed to address the numerous interests and abilities of a pre-K audience, but limitations exist with attention spans and gallery themes.
   Staff Time Requirements: 6 hours. Planning for the year's Itty Bitty Mornings takes about three hours, with additional time to prepare each event. Manning the event (setup, cleanup, and facilitation) requires another three hours per scheduled program.
   Audience Time Requirements: Flexible. Audience members have flexibility on the amount of time they spend on activities and themes, depending on interest, age, and ability.
   Scalability: ★★★ The Itty Bitty Morning activity is set up as stations within the larger museum gallery, allowing audience members to rotate through at their own pace. This model easily accommodates smaller audiences. However, larger audiences may need more stations to allow for flow. This is in addition to more materials, space, and staff.
   Analysis: There are several components that contribute to the success of the Itty Bitty Mornings program. Multiple activity stations are offered throughout the museum to invite participants to explore their interests. The targeted audience narrows selected interactives and crafts to focus on very specific skills and topics, allowing a deeper understanding and more concentrated connections. Finally, the museum opens early to accommodate preschoolers and their adults. This audience is free to explore museum spaces without the distractions and sometimes overwhelming presence of older children and other visitors. These programming components create a welcoming, targeted, accommodating environment catered to this preschool audience.

First Friday

City of Raleigh Museum, Raleigh, North Carolina
History Museum
Open House
  Target Audience: Children and families
  Attendance: 50–100 people

Figure 2.16 First Friday event at the City of Raleigh Museum

Overview: The first Friday of every month, the City of Raleigh Museum hosts free activities in downtown Raleigh. Hosted in conjunction with downtown Raleigh, the program takes advantage of the larger First Friday visitor traffic to invite families into the museum for refreshments, program activities, and events designed to engage audience members with the history and culture of the city. Artist demonstrations, new exhibit openings, crafts, and musical performances directed toward family audiences have all been featured during the three-hour open house.

Budget: $75

Interpretive Components: ★★★ The flexible nature of the program means the amount and depth of interpretive information shared depends on programming needs and audience interest.

Staff Time Requirements: ~5 hours/program. Time includes planning, coordinating event logistics, setup, manning the event, and cleanup.

Audience Time Requirements: Flexible. Participants are able to spend as much or as little time with the activity as they like.

Scalability: ★★★★★ Audience flexibility and program variability means this program model has the potential to handle as many participants as the space will allow.

Analysis: The City of Raleigh Museum is deliberate in coordinating their First Friday programming with that of the downtown Raleigh event. This larger event invites downtown businesses to offer special activities for the after-hours downtown audience. This attracts large groups of people to explore Raleigh's local businesses and organizations. The museum capitalizes on this to create engaging, family-oriented opportunities to explore the art and history of the community. Other museums can benefit from coordinating with a preexisting event, as the strategy reduces marketing costs while ensuring audience attendance. It also fosters community organizational networks and partnerships that can be leveraged for other museum needs.

Teddy Bear Tea

Cass County Historical Society, West Fargo, North Dakota
History Museum
Event

Target Audience: Children age 3 to 10 and their grandparents

Attendance: 25–50 people

Overview: Every Valentine's Day, the Cass County Historical Society hosts a Teddy Bear Tea event for children and their grandparents. The formal tea party includes using real china, tea sandwiches, scones, cakes, tea, and lemonade. Over tea, participants are encouraged to socialize and spend time together. They are even invited to bring a favorite stuffed animal or doll to join them for the party.

Budget: $85

Interpretive Components: ★ While the Victorian tea party is the inspiration for the event, the focus is on guest conversations and dialogue, not interpretation. This social collaboration builds communication skills while strengthening familial ties.

Staff Time Requirements: ~9 hours. This event requires a good bit of setup and cleanup in addition to hosting the party.

Audience Time Requirements: ~1 hour. The tea party runs for an hour.

Scalability: ★★★ The Teddy Bear Tea would work best with a set attendance number based on the abilities and limitations of the host organization. Larger groups would need more tables, snacks, staff, and so on. To this end, reservations are likely the best method to ensure event and audience needs are met.

Analysis: The Teddy Bear Tea is unique in that it directly targets child/grandparent groups rather than traditional family audiences. Instead of focusing on interpretation and museum activities, the event is designed to encourage discussion and interaction between family members. To successfully accomplish this, the museum must be willing to step back and allow attendees to direct the program based on their individual needs and interests. While the program creates a memorable environment, participant experiences are directed on personal interactions. Museums interested in duplicating this programming goal must be willing to relinquish certain responsibilities to the audience themselves.

Playdate: Happy Birthday, Trees!

Skirball Cultural Center, Los Angeles, California
Cultural Center
Event

Target Audience: Preschool children and adults

Attendance: 25–50 people

Overview: Although part of a larger Playdate series, Happy Birthday, Trees! was celebrated with the Jewish holiday of Tu B'Shevat (the New Year of the Trees). Selected activities associated with trees and conservation include fruit tastings, art activities, and a story time designed to educate preschool participants on both the biology and function of trees as well as conservation efforts. This approach provides age-appropriate interpretation while fostering curiosity and creative development.

Budget: $91

Photograph by BeBe Jacobs.
Courtesy of Skirball Cultural Center

Figure 2.17 Skirball Playdate: Happy Birthday, Trees! at the Skirball Cultural Center

Interpretive Components: ★★★★ Staff educators plan the activities specifically for a pre-K audience and their adults while covering multiple interpretive aspects of trees and arbor conservation.

Staff Time Requirements: ~15 hours. Staff plan, develop, and teach the program. This includes prep time, research, and cleanup.

Audience Time Requirements: 1.5 hours. The event includes a circle time discussion, themed activities, and a story time. This requires an extended stay to participate in all event components.

Scalability: ★★ The program is capped at 20 child–adult pairs meaning a total of 40 participants. This cap ensures a relatively intimate experience. Larger audiences would not be guaranteed the same level of engagement.

Analysis: Happy Birthday, Trees! uses the Tu B'Shevat Jewish holiday to inspire program development. Although program components don't necessarily include holiday interpretation, its presence is acknowledged and expanded to provide age-appropriate content. The Skirball Cultural Center's mission speaks to traditions of Jewish hospitality blended with American ideals of freedom and equality. Tu B'Shevat fits within this mission while allowing elements of biology and conservation—concepts not immediately evident in the Skirball's goals. This illustrates that program diversity and flexibility can be guided by an organization's mission statement, not hampered by it. Missions are vital to organizational operations, as they define who and what operational goals are, and they offer creative direction and inspiration to expand successful programming efforts. Local history museums can find scientific and artist discussions using local and visiting characters as inspiration. Art museums can explore engineering and mathematics through studies of perspective and architecture. Programs should be varied and wide ranging, but they must also make sense in relation to organizational missions.

Gold Panning

National Mining Hall of Fame and Museum, Leadville, Colorado
History Museum
Activity-Based/Partnership
Target Audience: Children and families
Attendance: 50–100 people

Figure 2.18 Gold Panning at the National Mining Hall of Fame and Museum

Overview: Gold Panning is an outdoor activity that simulates the historic gold panning process. Using metal washtubs, gold pans, water, and small vials, participants are taught how to manipulate the pans to wash away excess dirt and sand to get to the desired minerals. Vials are used to collect any mineral or "glittery stuff" so it can be taken home. The activity introduces historic concepts and contexts while exploring creative problem-solving techniques and hands-on interactions. It provides an experience-based approach to this mining process.

Budget: ~$100

Interpretive Components: ★★ While the activity's focus is specifically on the process of gold panning, historic information is often shared during the procedure.

Staff Time Requirements: ~3–4 hours. Preparation and planning time is roughly one hour, but the activity can operate for hours at a time. The largest amount of time may be spent finding an appropriate matrix for the event. The National Mining Hall of Fame and Museum has fostered a partnership with a mining educational foundation to provide theirs for free.

Audience Time Requirements: Flexible. Participants can be flexible in the amount of time they spend with the activity. A single attempt may take only five minutes, but the opportunity to spend extended amounts of time panning is entirely possible.

Scalability: ★★★ The activity is fairly easy to scale either larger or smaller. It can be done with a single tub, one or two pans, and one volunteer, or it can be expanded to multiple volunteers, tubs, and pans, depending on resources and space.

Analysis: The Gold Panning program concentrates on a single activity to provide a unique programming experience. This activity-based model may appear too narrow a focus and possibly limit interpretation opportunities, but the reverse is true. The process seems simple enough, but it hides a surprising amount of work and practice to provide varying layers of complexity and information to explore. By using this singular focus, the National Mining Hall of Fame and Museum encourages participants to apply their whole attention to this historic process. Gaining firsthand knowledge of how to pan, the movements (and aches) involved, and the small but exciting reward of ore provides a deeper understanding of historic gold miners and adds context to larger historic mining narratives. Related activity-based programs can offer similar success for other museums.

Family Painting Workshop

Evansville African American Museum, Evansville, Indiana
Art/Culture Museum
Workshop

Target Audience: Family groups

Attendance: 50–100 people

Overview: The Evansville African American Museum's Family Painting Workshop encourages families to make art together while exploring

African American art and cultural themes. Each session combines mini-lectures, gallery visits to examine displayed pieces, and hands-on painting instruction. Families learn about African American artists and art movements while being taught painting methods. This combines family collaboration and cooperative learning with formal art instruction.

Budget: $100

Interpretive Components: ★★★★★ This workshop combines staff-led instruction with examining source materials and personal artistic interpretations to explore African American art history. Participants are able to apply concepts and methods to create personal paintings to keep.

Staff Time Requirements: ~13 hours. Each workshop requires time to create sample paintings, workshop prep, and cleanup, in addition to manning the event. Groups of more than 30 people require a second staff person.

Audience Time Requirements: ~2.5 hours. Workshops run between two and three hours, depending on the complexity and breadth of the topic.

Scalability: ★★★ While the workshop size can be adjusted depending on space capabilities and material availability, larger groups would not only require additional staffing, but they would also expand the materials budget over the $100 mark.

Analysis: This workshop is specifically designed for family groups rather than for children with an accompanying adult. It simultaneously provides in-depth instruction for both children and their families while exploring complex topics. This creates a challenging interpretive situation, as instruction must be both age and ability appropriate. However, encouraging families to create art together can be a great way to introduce new and complex themes to younger audiences while fostering social collaboration. This deepens subject understandings while strengthening family ties. Museums seeking a similar workshop structure should find subjects equally appealing to children and their adults to ensure unified interest while designing instruction to encourage teamwork.

Victorian Christmas

Moody Museum, Taylor, Texas
Historic Site
Open House

Target Audience: Kindergarten through grade 4 students and their families

Attendance: 25–50 people

Credit: Moody Museum

*Figure 2.19 Moody Museum board member Julia O'Bryan Lieb
helps a child create a Santa image from the child's handprint.
Miss Lieb dressed in a period costume for the event
and found that the children were quite intrigued by her attire.*

Overview: Every year in early December, the Moody Museum invites local students in kindergarten through fourth grade and their families. Students are able to make Victorian-themed ornaments, families are encouraged to take tours of the historic house, and groups are able to take Christmas photos in front of the decorated tree. The event offers students and families the chance to explore the historic site, learn about Victorian Christmas traditions, and create original take-home crafts.

Budget: $100

Interpretive Components: ★★★★ This open house-event presents Victorian history in an age-appropriate, interactive, and relatable environment. Families are able to explore the site's history within the understanding of their own holiday traditions.

Staff Time Requirements: 4 hours. Time includes preparation, setup, manning the event, and cleanup.

Audience Time Requirements: ~1 hour. While the event runs for two hours, most families are able to complete their activities in under an hour.

Scalability: ★★★★ The biggest limitation on audience size is the space. Many facilities, such as the Moody Museum, have smaller rooms, making it difficult to host such activities. However, if the space is available, the program structure can accommodate large numbers fairly easily.

Analysis: The Victorian Christmas event is an on-site program that specifically targets elementary students and their families, welcoming them to the historic site. Explicitly inviting students within a selected grade range allows age-appropriate interpretation and activities while expressing an interest and desire to reach those students. Participants are given the impression that the event is directly for them, fostering a friendly and personal museum–audience relationship. Working for this specified audience further benefits by focusing the museum's marketing and planning efforts without the restrictions of a formal school program. Any museum can adapt similar program methods to target and attract this specified audience.

Kids Dig

Wyoming Dinosaur Center, Thermopolis, Wyoming
Science Museum
Off-Site

   Target Audience: Children

   Attendance: 10–25 people

   Overview: Kids Dig provides children the opportunity to survey, excavate, and analyze dinosaur fossils. Participants are transported to a working paleontology excavation site to spend several hours prospecting for and excavating fossils. The day-long program concludes with prepping bones in the lab and creating replica casts. Audience members are supervised by trained professionals, and within program boundaries, they are allowed a certain amount of autonomy to work the site.

   Budget: $100

   Interpretive Components: ★★★★★ This program provides an immersive, hands-on experience for every level of paleontological interest. In addition to site tools and processes, participants learn about specific dinosaurs, geologic formations, and paleoenvironments as they relate to that particular excavation.

Figure 2.20 Kids Dig at the Wyoming Dinosaur Center

Staff Time Requirements: ~40 hours. This is a very staff-heavy program, as multiple museum representatives must stay with participants throughout the day. This is in addition to monitoring them in the lab setting and providing instruction. Planning, setup, and cleanup time must also be considered.

Audience Time Requirements: 7 hours. This is a full, day-long program that runs from 9:00 a.m. to 4:00 p.m. Transportation is provided.

Scalability: ★★ This program works best with smaller groups. Larger participant numbers put more stress on staff, transportation, and supplies.

Analysis: The Kids Dig program inserts children directly into a real-world excavation site. They are given on-the-job training, and their assistance is acknowledged on the same level as college students and adult volunteers. This not only provides participants with an authentic, hands-on experience, but it also provides volunteers to help with on-site operations. While the allure of a dinosaur excavation can be hard to duplicate, other museums can experiment with programs that invite children to take part in genuine field activities and environments. Similar programs have the potential to grow participant confidence levels as well as positive connections to the chosen field and the museum.

Mornings at the Museum

Museum of Peoples and Cultures at Brigham Young University, Provo, Utah
History/Culture Museum
In-Gallery
    Target Audience: Children age 5 to 11 and accompanying adult
    Attendance: 100–200 people

*Figure 2.21 Mornings at the Museum at the Museum of Peoples and Cultures
at Brigham Young University*

Overview: Over the summer, the Museum of Peoples and Cultures offers themed program activities for children ages 5 through 11 and an accompanying adult. Each week's theme is offered twice per week over a three-week period in July. All themes are chosen based on the museum's mission, exhibits, and educational resources. Archaeology, homes around the world, pottery, and cultural traditions have all been explored through hands-on activities, objects, and gallery discussions. Many times, the Mornings at the Museum program even takes an alternate perspective than that offered through the exhibit text.

Budget: $100

Interpretive Components: ★★★★ Mornings at the Museum uses a variety of activity types and historic perspectives to provide quality, engaging summer learning. Museum galleries and education collections are utilized to get children familiar with the museum's role and to encourage different ways of thinking about history.

Staff Time Requirements: ~35 hours. Each week's theme requires several hours to plan and prepare, in addition to leading each session twice a week.

Audience Time Requirements: ~1 hour. Mornings at the Museum sessions run a little over an hour to ensure each child is engaged and given the opportunity to participate with all program components.

Scalability: ★★★ Each session is capped at about 20 children to guarantee a good staff–visitor ratio. Larger groups would need additional staff or more scheduled times. This could put additional strains on the staff and facilities.

Analysis: Mornings at the Museum differs from other pop-up, in-gallery programs in two distinct ways. First, while the program may utilize preestablished teaching resources, it often deliberately approaches these topics using alternative perspectives. This actively challenges many participant understandings and encourages broader discussions to explore the implications of these presented views. Other museums looking to duplicate this program should be ready to explore their collection and correlating museum themes through alternative lenses and be comfortable exploring these perspectives with child audiences.

Second, rather than the more common "one-and-done" approach, each program in the Mornings at the Museum series is designed to be presented twice. This requires twice the preparation, setup, cleanup, and facilitation and can affect theme and activity options based on fitting this need. However, the twice-weekly program ensures additional audience reach and provides a certain amount of participant flexibility, as they are able to select which program they can attend. Providing this simple service is not only recognized but also appreciated by audience members. Museums looking to create new programs could profit from similar considerations.

Lulie Crawford Wildflowers and Watercolors

Tread of Pioneers Museum, Steamboat Springs, Colorado
History Museum
Workshop/Partnership
   Target Audience: Children interested in art
   Attendance: 10–25 people

Figure 2.22 Exploring wildflowers with Lulie Crawford's Wildflowers and Watercolors
at the Tread of Pioneers Museum

Overview: The Tread of Pioneers Museum uses the life and art of pioneer Lulie Crawford to explore local history, art, and science with local children. Participants learn about the life and artwork of the artist, particularly her wildflower watercolors. They are able to tour the local botanical park and then learn how to paint wildflowers from a professional artist. These paintings are available to take home at the program's conclusion.

   Budget: $100

   Interpretive Components: ★★★★★ This program uses a multidisciplinary approach that combines history, local lore, art, botany, and biology in a single program focusing on artist Lulie Crawford.

   Staff Time Requirements: 10 hours. The Wildflowers and Watercolors program requires about six hours of prep and marketing and two hours for two people to implement the workshop.

Audience Time Requirements: 1 hour. Program components take about an hour to complete. This includes workshop instruction and the botanical garden visit.

Scalability: ★★★ This program works best with smaller groups to ensure engagement and proper artistic instruction. Larger groups would require significantly more materials, staff, and time.

Analysis: The Lulie Crawford Wildflowers and Watercolors program uses a single character to inspire a multidisciplinary approach to art, history, and botany, among other fields, but it extends this inspiration to incorporate several outside partnerships to greatly increase the program's experiential value. Not only does the Tread of Pioneers Museum work with the local botanical garden to hold the workshop and provide first-hand examination opportunities for wildflowers, but they also enlist the instruction of a professional watercolor artist to lead the painting portion of the program. This provides participants with a relevant and immersive environment while allowing them to learn from a recognized expert in the program's field. Many museums should be open to similar partnerships to enhance their workshop offerings and increase participant satisfaction.

NOTE

1 Freeman Tilden, *Interpreting Our Heritage* (Chapel Hill: University of North Carolina Press, 2007).

3

Programming for Teens
and Young Adults

For many museums, the most difficult audience to consistently reach are those between the ages of 14 and 23. Teenagers and college-age museum-goers are seeking decidedly different experiences than many museums are prepared to administer or even know how to provide. Because of the challenges associated with this audience, numerous museums have written them off as unreachable and don't even attempt to draw them into gallery spaces.

Today's Gen Z and Millennial audiences want an open and transparent place where they are free to express themselves while learning from those around them. They want autonomy to explore the crazy, cool collection only offered through the museum, and they need the flexibility to become involved in ways that fit into their busy schedules. Personal relevance is key, and the opportunity to share these personal connections grounds them in the museum space. Even more, as digital natives, they want to stay connected beyond the museum buildings.

To reach this audience, museums must be prepared to drop their "expert" position and take on a more guiding or mentorship role. They need to consider allowing teens and young adults to take ownership of the museum in such a way to encourage their investment in the collection through personal connections and experiences—all while providing multiple avenues of involvement and streams of digital connectivity.

The programs included here reach today's teen and young adult audience using multiple programming models, but they are each successful in drawing this audience into the museum in engaging ways. Programs span social media accounts, volunteer opportunities, school programming, open work areas, and even contests.

SOCIAL MEDIA

Social media programming can be intimidating for museum staff not familiar with digital platforms, but the potential for opening the museum to new, international audiences, especially those in this age group, cannot be ignored. The key is finding the platform that best fits the organization's abilities. To be successful, accounts must be active, including regular posts, follower interaction, and conversation follow-ups. This requires dedicated, daily staff time, planning, and maintenance.

The Georgia Museum of Art and the Museum of Latin American Art have analyzed their museum activities and staffing availabilities to choose Snapchat and Tumblr accounts, respectively, for engagement. Each platform has different capabilities in reaching their followers. While Snapchat appeals to an audience who only wants brief glimpses into the museum's world, Tumblr allows for more detailed discussion and analysis while encouraging follower responses and conversations. Both provide digital content that's available whenever the audience wants access while still giving the freedom to consume the information at whatever depth is desired.

VOLUNTEER OPPORTUNITIES

Offering volunteer opportunities may seem like the easiest way to meet teen and young adult programming needs, but they can be incredibly time consuming without a guaranteed volunteer return. Still, when well managed, they can also be exceedingly successful. Inviting young adults into museum workspaces to specifically help them build professional skills, such as the Penn Museum's Teen Summer Internships, provides a much-needed service, but it requires large amounts of staff time to train and supervise each participant. However, allowing volunteers the autonomy to study and incorporate their own interests into their duties, whether through tours like the Williams College Museum of Art's Student Choice program or through family program presentations like the Skirball Cultural Center's Teen Corps, encourages deeper engagement and interaction with regular museum attendees while ensuring a stronger volunteer–museum investment and commitment. This can translate to longer volunteer terms as well as a dedicated future audience as the teens and young adults grow.

SCHOOL PROGRAMS

Developing programming specific to formal young adult class groups seems a simple extension of primary and middle school programming, but it can be definitively more complicated. In addition to tying program content to necessary standards of learning, program design must take into account fractured class schedules, higher cognitive content, and 21st-Century Skills. To accommodate these challenges, many high school– and college-targeted programs are split over multiple visits. Such is the case with Carbon County Museum's Rawlins History Hunt, Agecroft Hall's Shakespeare at Agecroft, and Shadows-on-the-Teche's Purchased Lives Workshop.

But while each of these programs is designed for school groups over multiple visits, they serve very different educational goals. The Rawlins History Hunt helps students become familiar with local history and community engagement, and the Purchased Lives Workshop uses site-specific primary documents to explore slavery's impact on historic and contemporary community landscapes. Shakespeare at Agecroft not only explores Shakespeare's historic context, but it also even goes so far as to have student participants stage their own production.

WORKSPACE OPPORTUNITIES

Two hallmarks of attracting this unique audience are providing social hangout spaces and encouraging self-directed learning. The Children's Museum of Pittsburgh combines these components in their Youth Make program. The museum offers their staffed makerspace as a safe place to explore artistic expression and practice creative methods and processes through collaborations with both peers and museum staff. Allowing participant autonomy and project ownership nurtures audience growth, both through skills development and personal relevancy.

CONTESTS

Friendly competition is a well-known component of teens and young adults, and it can be successfully leveraged for programming success when combined with other education or programmatic goals. For the Harn Museum of Art, their Words on Canvas contest demands deep understandings of collection pieces expressed through unique creative prose. Contest winners are offered exposure and recognition on the college level through the display and public reading of their work.

PROGRAMS FOR TEENS AND YOUNG ADULTS

With programs like the Skirball Cultural Center's Teen Corps volunteer group and the Children's Museum of Pittsburgh's Youth Make, museums are ditching the traditional museum program and reaching out to this unique and rewarding audience to establish a dedicated museum audience.

Snapchat Account

Georgia Museum of Art, Athens, Georgia
Art Museum
Social Media
   Target Audience: Teens and college students
   Attendance: More than 200 people
   Overview: The Georgia Museum of Art's Snapchat account serves dual purposes. While staff use it to relay behind-the-scenes glimpses and information on collection pieces, visitors are encouraged to share their museum experiences using the app within museum galleries. The brief posts are designed to appeal to younger audiences and explore the art museum, its role, and its collection. Posts further illustrate the museum's online presence and spur digital followers to share their own museum Snapchat stories.
   Budget: $0
   Interpretive Components: ★★ Snapchat posts are brief and expire after 24 hours, so the opportunities to interpret are very limited. Still, the ability to pare an art museum experience to a 10-second "story" can allow for a greater reach and more interaction with audience members. The simple, short life of the social media format gives a sense of exclusivity and encourages followers to explore more information.
   Staff Time Requirements: 15 minutes/week. Planning and developing a post only takes a few minutes, but posts should be made several times a week.
   Audience Time Requirements: Variable. Because no Snapchat "story" can be more than 10 seconds long, audience members must only commit to short time periods. Once the audience has seen a post, they are free to move on or visit the museum's other online platforms for more information.
   Scalability: ★★★★★ Because the amount of posting effort is the same whether one person sees it or hundreds see it, this program is infinitely scalable.
   Analysis: Museums have access to numerous digital social media platforms, but they must choose the ones that best meet their needs. For the Georgia Museum of Art, Snapchat's ability to share personal, appealing content with little staff effort makes it ideal for collection and program-

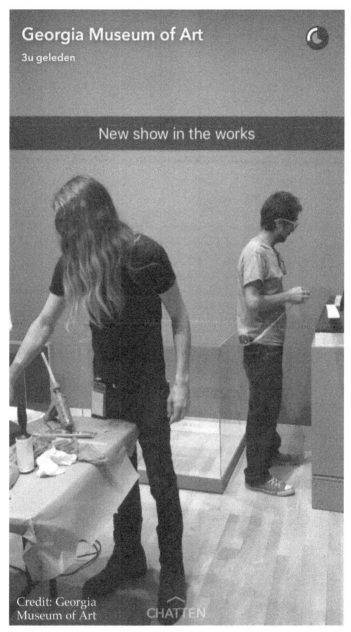

Figure 3.1 The Georgia Museum of Art's Snapchat account

matic interaction. When paired with the platform's growing market, it becomes a fun, easy method of digital engagement available to an untold, international youth audience. Snapchat accounts are free, so any museum willing to commit the time to make frequent posts can duplicate this effort. Snap stories can equally include object conservation, exhibit installation, staff questions, and visitor interactions.

Student Choice

Williams College Museum of Art, Williamstown, Massachusetts
Art Museum
Tour/Volunteer
   Target Audience: College students
   Attendance: 10–25 people
   Overview: The Student Choice program brings student gallery guides into the museum to design their own tours around individual interests. Student-planned tours focus on one to two concepts of personal interest to the guide and explore the selected topic through the lens of the museum's collection. After a short training session that includes tour teaching methods, curator-led exhibition discussions, and time to personalize individual tours, guides are equipped to lead up to 20 people through museum galleries.
   Budget: $0
   Interpretive Components: ★★★ Students are able to use curator-provided information to make their own relevant connections with displayed artwork. These connections are then incorporated into their individualized tours.
   Staff Time Requirements: ~48+ hours. The 1.5-hour staff-led training is held weekly during the 16-week academic school year. This does not include planning and program development time.
   Audience Time Requirements: ~20 hours. In addition to the 1.5-hour training, student gallery guides commit to 30-minute or hour-long shifts every Saturday.
   Scalability: ★★★ The Student Choice program could accommodate as many student gallery guides as the museum is willing to train and manage. Once students complete the training, they are ready to lead their individually developed tours.
   Analysis: The Student Choice volunteer program not only offers students the chance to be involved with museum operations, but it also provides the unique opportunity to use museum-developed skills to create their own, individualized tour programs. Allowing students this chance builds their program and communication skills while growing their commitment and investment in the museum organization. Additionally, it affords the museum access to new interpretation from differing viewpoints that can be incorporated into existing interpretive efforts. While

Figure 3.2 Student Choice Tours at the Williams College Museum of Art

the benefits of establishing a similar program can be found for both volunteer participants and the museum, it is accomplished with a significant time commitment. Museums looking to duplicate the Student Choice program must be willing to dedicate that necessary time to train and develop volunteer skills in order for any personalized tours to succeed.

Tumblr Account

Museum of Latin American Art, Long Beach, California
Art Museum
Social Media
   Target Audience: Teens and college students
   Attendance: More than 200 people

Credit: Museum of Latin American Art

Figure 3.3 The Museum of Latin American Art's Tumblr account

Overview: The Museum of Latin American Art's Tumblr account provides unique glimpses into the permanent collection while boosting the exposure of emerging artists and discussing relevant program initiatives. These posts are immediately viewable to account subscribers and are also searchable on the internet for the international public. Tumblr's easy-to-use platform removes audience viewing barriers and allows subscribers to quickly comment and share each post exponentially.

Budget: $0

Interpretive Components: ★★★★ Account posts can cover a wide range of interpretive material, including artist's backgrounds, artistic styles, processes, and historical context. Posts can be as lengthy as necessary to communicate the information.

Staff Time Requirements: 20 minutes/week. Posts usually take a few minutes a day to plan and develop, but three to four posts should be scheduled per week.

Audience Time Requirements: Variable. Audience members can spend a few seconds or several minutes on each post, depending on their interest level.

Scalability: ★★★★★ The amount of staff effort is the same, whether for an audience of 1 or an audience of 3,000.

Analysis: Digital users crave the open communication today's social media platforms provide, and Tumblr offers easy, seamless interaction between the account host and content subscribers. In fact, an argument could be made that the success of this Museum of Latin American Art effort is dependent on these museum–audience conversations. Interpretive content is valuable and drives the digital engagement, but viewing it is only half of a Tumblr user's goal. They seek consistent communication and input. Museums looking to take advantage of Tumblr's free accounts must take this into consideration.

Purchased Lives Workshop

Shadows-on-the-Teche, New Iberia, Louisiana
Historic Site
Tour/Partnership Workshop
    Target Audience: Teens
    Attendance: 25–50 people
    Overview: The Purchased Lives Workshop encourages students to explore the impact of the slave trade. Beginning with a contextual tour of the Purchased Lives traveling exhibit and continuing with program components at the antebellum plantation Shadows-on-the-Teche, students use primary sources, both from the exhibit and from the historic site's archival collection, to critically analyze the history, effects, and influence of slavery in the New Orleans region. They learn to place these sources in context and to ask questions left unanswered.
    Budget: $10

Interpretive Components: ★★★ This workshop uses multiple sites and collections exposure to develop a deeper understanding of the institution of slavery. Through the active use of historic documents, students gain research experience through trusted, primary sources.

Staff Time Requirements: ~2 hours. Time includes tours at both sites, setup, and cleanup.

Audience Time Requirements: 1.5 hours. Each tour and activity time runs roughly 45 minutes.

Scalability: ★★ Smaller groups allow deeper discussion and more intimate engagement with the material. Larger groups not only cut into this interaction, but they also are more difficult to move through the limited tour spaces.

Analysis: While the Purchased Lives Workshop focuses on documents associated with New Orleans slavery, the idea of working with primary sources and archival materials to examine historic context and lingering effects of past practices and events can form strong youth programming options. Engaging with authentic materials helps build research and critical thinking skills while developing deeper understandings of current institutions and events. Numerous topics lend themselves to this programming model and can support similar programming efforts. Exploring the native reservation period informs on contemporary economic dispersal. Studying the 1863 New York Draft Riots builds understanding on today's immigration debates. Looking at the motivations behind Red Scare actions creates context for current international politics. Organizations with access to archival collections can find their own relevant themes for youth to explore.

Rawlins History Hunt

Carbon County Museum, Rawlins, Wyoming
History Museum
School
   Target Audience: Local high school students
   Attendance: 10–25 people
   Overview: The Rawlins History Hunt encourages teens to explore local history through a semiguided scavenger hunt. Students first visit the museum with specific program questions to become familiar with local characters, history, and themes and how they inform on national historic narratives. Working in groups, they are then transported to the local main street to match these concepts with specific historic sites in the downtown area. To get credit for finding a site, they must provide a selfie of them at the site in question. Depending on resources, the first group to identify all sites receives a prize.

Budget: $15

Interpretive Components: ★★★★ The Rawlins History Hunt introduces multiple local historic concepts within the national historic narrative and helps students connect these themes with sites in their own community.

Staff Time Requirements: 10 hours. Time to plan, develop, and manage program components are included.

Audience Time Requirements: 2 hours. This time is split between the museum visit and exploring the downtown community sites.

Scalability: ★★★ The Rawlins History Hunt works best with a single class. More students would take more staff and time to work through the program, while smaller groups would not have the same opportunities to collaborate.

Analysis: The Rawlins History Hunt takes advantage of community history to help students tie familiar sites with larger themes within US history. Using the museum space to provide context helps orient participants to program components and illustrates the museum's role in sharing local stories, and providing time downtown opens students to the value and history of their community. While the current program best fits a local history museum, the ability to connect museum themes with community features can be adapted in numerous ways. Public art concepts; architectural and engineering features; scientific processes; and, of course, historic connections can all be explored using this program model.

Teen Summer Internships

Penn Museum, Philadelphia, Pennsylvania
History Museum
Volunteer

Target Audience: Teens

Attendance: 10–25 people

Overview: The Teen Summer Internships is a three-week, unpaid internship program that brings teenagers into the back halls of the museum. Each intern works with a museum staff supervisor to help with museum-based projects. These tailored projects, partnered with direct supervision by professional museum staff, provide opportunities to develop both professional and personal skill sets. Each program group includes a two-hour session with the program supervisor going over museum processes, programming components, and general training. The remainder of the session (approximately three hours) is spent with individual departmental supervisors to work on the assigned project.

Budget: $50

Credit: Penn Museum

Figure 3.4 Teen Summer Internships at the Penn Museum

Interpretive Components: ★★★ Interns are given unique access to the museum, its collections, and its programs. Working in a specified department helps them develop professional and personal skills while assisting with departmental projects.

Staff Time Requirements: ~600 hours total. This total requirement is a little misleading, in that it includes the preparation, marketing, and management of the program coordinator (~110 hours) in addition to the time administered by each intern's supervisor (~50 hours per supervisor).

Audience Time Requirements: 90 hours. Students are with either the project coordinator or their supervisor for six hours a day, five days a week, for three weeks.

Scalability: ★★ The number of interns is directly dependent on staff willingness and availability to supervise. There should be a one-to-one ratio of staff to intern.

Analysis: The Teen Summer Internships are dually focused on volunteers building professional skills while providing assistance for projects throughout the museum. The short program time frame allows staff to focus volunteer involvement on specific departmental tasks and skills development while offering volunteers a glimpse into operational duties and work behind the scenes. It is recognized that this program model requires a monumental time commitment from both staff and participants to be successful, but this commitment can pay off by developing a trained volunteer base dedicated to the museum. Museums looking to duplicate this model must have staff-wide buy-in and be willing to devote the necessary time for training and program management. It should also be noted that, to foster a diverse intern pool, it may be necessary to provide additional program perks (e.g., transportation, food, stipends) that would significantly increase program costs.

Shakespeare at Agecroft

Agecroft Hall, Richmond, Virginia
Historic House
School/Tour

Target Audience: High school English classes

Attendance: 25–50 people

Overview: Shakespeare at Agecroft uses the atmosphere of the historic site's Tudor mansion to explore Shakespearian plays and the history and context surrounding them. Beginning with a tour of the museum, followed by a discussion of Elizabethan entertainment and theater, students become familiar with Elizabethan theatrical motivations and processes before they stage a Shakespearian scene preselected by their teachers. The program allows students to learn about actors' roles, technician duties, and audience experiences firsthand.

Budget: $55

Interpretive Components: ★★★★ This program provides a unique look at Elizabethan theater and the world of Shakespeare while giving students the hands-on opportunity to produce and stage a scene from a play they've read in the classroom.

Staff Time Requirements: ~6 hours. Because of the varying components of this program, multiple staff members are required. This is in addition to any planning, setup, and cleanup.

Audience Time Requirements: 2.5 hours. Students are on-site for nearly three hours to participate in all program components. This includes the tour, discussion, and scene staging.

Scalability: ★★★ This program works best with up to 50 students and can easily be adapted for less. However, a larger group would require more staff and a longer visit.

Analysis: This program uses a unique approach to explore classroom-based themes. The historic site offers a multidisciplinary tactic to combine literature, history, and the performing arts while directly involving students in the lesson. The site visit creates an immersive atmosphere to better understand the context and limitations of Shakespeare's work, and the guided staged scene permits students to apply these understandings first-hand. While Agecroft Hall is able to leverage their site to examine Shakespeare, the concept of combining museum themes with the performing arts can create amazing multidiscipinary teaching opportunities. Historic, artistic, and scientific themes can be explored through the unique character perspectives and sites associated with those stories. Museums willing to develop these connections can see similar programming success.

Teen Corps

Skirball Cultural Center, Los Angeles, California
Cultural Center
Volunteer
   Target Audience: Teens
   Attendance: 50–100 people
   Overview: The Teen Corps program brings teenagers into the Family Programs Department to gain exposure to the museum field and to experience working with visitors in the museum. They learn to facilitate programs and engage children in the museum galleries. Teens are allowed to weave their personal interests into these experiential presentations. This allows them to present the museum from their perspective.
   Budget: $95
   Interpretive Components: ★★★★ Participants are exposed to the inner workings of the museum, including different presentation styles, how to recognize audience prior experiences, and the design and development of exhibits. They are encouraged to learn how their personal interests fit into the larger picture of the organization and how to share that perspective with visitors, specifically children and their families.
   Staff Time Requirements: ~60 hours. This time includes planning, recruitment, conducting interviews, training, and general supervision and volunteer coordination.
   Audience Time Requirements: ~25 hours. After a short personal interview and appropriate training, volunteer participants sign up for four-hour shifts. There is no requirement for how many shifts they must complete.
   Scalability: ★★★ The Teen Corps program can be scaled for as many volunteers as museum staff can handle. With staff availability, potentially hundreds of volunteers can be selected and trained. It could be just as viable for only a handful to be used.
   Analysis: The Skirball Cultural Center's Teen Corps program centers on training youth to develop and present family programs. This focus allows volunteers to develop extensive presentation skills and gain considerable experience in working with a variety of child ages and abilities.

For many participants, this experience can build foundations for future careers in education; child development; social work; and, of course, museums. In addition, museum staff are able to take advantage of volunteer programming efforts to develop new programs and strengthen existing program options. This program can be adapted for any museum, regardless of mission, location, or staff size, as long as staff are willing to train and supervise the volunteers.

Words on Canvas

Harn Museum of Art, Gainesville, Florida
Art Museum
Contest
   Target Audience: College students
   Attendance: 50–100 people
   Overview: Words on Canvas is a writing competition for college students to create original poetry inspired by the museum's art collection. Poetry is submitted to a judging panel, and winning prose is presented at an evening event each spring. These pieces are then temporarily displayed with their corresponding art piece in the museum.
   Budget: $100
   Interpretive Components: ★★★ While museum interpretation may be limited, participating students are able to share personal interpretations of their chosen pieces. This provides relevant connections for both participants and regular museum visitors.
   Staff Time Requirements: ~20 hours. Because the budget is used wholly to provide prizes, staff time must include arranging volunteer judges as well as organizing and tracking entries.
   Audience Time Requirements: ~2 hours. Participants are free to spend as much time on their entries as necessary. Audience members at the final presentation event usually stay about 30 minutes.
   Scalability: ★★★★★ Once the prizes are set, the contest can support any number of entries. The biggest commitment for a larger entry pool is the amount of time needed to judge the submissions.
   Analysis: Museum-sponsored contests elicit submissions that offer new perspectives on museum collection pieces. They have the potential to involve previously unreached audiences, drawing them into gallery spaces and encouraging their feedback. This presents the museum as an inclusive and open organization that welcomes and even celebrates differing perspectives.
   Although Words on Canvas is designed around art pieces, this program model could be potentially adapted for either history or science museum exhibits as well.

Youth Make

Children's Museum of Pittsburgh, Pittsburgh, Pennsylvania
Children's Museum
Activity-Based/Social Club
   Target Audience: Preteens and teens
   Attendance: Less than 10 people
   Overview: The monthly Youth Make hangouts allow preteens and teens to explore the materials, tools, and processes of an artist's makerspace by working on projects of their choosing. Using the museum's established community workspace, participants share the creative area with professional and community artists while learning artistic methods through first-hand experience.
   Budget: $100
   Interpretive Components: ★★★ Because participants work on their own projects or inventions, inquiries and interpretation are limited to those components directly related to these projects. However, the hands-on, practical applications can offer stronger interpretive ties.
   Staff Time Requirements: ~2 hours/session. Youth Make uses dedicated maker staff already involved in the museum's artistic workspace to facilitate programming components. This means additional staff time is minimal.
   Audience Time Requirements: 2 hours/month. Youth Make hangouts run about two hours a month.
   Scalability: ★★ This program is dependent on a low staff–participant ratio (1:7 at the most). This means larger groups require a larger staff pool and more materials.
   Analysis: Providing a safe, welcoming space for youth to explore creative processes can fulfill a community need. Such facilities can improve audience perceptions of the museum by turning it into a place for free expression, where instruction between fledgling creatives and professional artists is commonplace. However, programs like Youth Make are only possible with a preexisting artist makerspace and dedicated maker educators. Without this space, costs and logistical concerns increase exponentially.

4

Programming for Adults

Adult audiences are one of the most important visitor groups for the museum field. They can come on their own or as part of a larger, intergenerational group when they bring their children, teens, and even elders with them. While they are a common audience type, museums often overlook their unique programming needs. Many times, adults are taken for granted, grouped into the "general public" and not identified as a focused target audience deserving of their own programming efforts. But to ignore this audience is to potentially miss the biggest and most influential audience group available.

In the museum field, adults are seen as the most general visitor, but they seek specific experiences unique to their situation. Many adults want museum encounters that acknowledge their independence and individuality, and they want the freedom to follow their museum interests on their schedules. They enjoy the opportunity to use museum spaces in nonmuseum formats. They want adult themes, and they want to have fun while they share them with their friends and partners.

To satisfy this audience's craving for such different experiences, museums must offer flexible programming (think open-house or on-demand options) while providing a social space to share experiences and conversations. Museums should be willing to partner with nonmuseum entities and provide space for these gatherings, and museums can't be afraid of adult beverages and themes that stretch into the "naughty" and unexpected.

OPEN HOUSES

Open-house events offer museums the opportunity to share services, programs, and exhibits while allowing visitors the freedom and flexibility to move through the space on their own, gravitating to parts that attract their interest and eschewing areas that don't. These open programs can appeal to many audience types, or they can target a specific group. The

Battle of Franklin Trust's Teacher Appreciation Day and the National Museum of Women in the Arts' Member Preview Day take this approach, but while they both target adult, community audiences, their goals in doing so are incredibly different. The Teacher Appreciation Day open house offers local teachers the chance to sample programs and educational opportunities offered by the sites and museums of the trust, while the Member Preview Day opens new National Museum of Women in the Arts exhibit spaces for members to explore and experience.

EXTRAEXPERIENTIAL TOURS

Tours are a great way for museums to share their unique collections and the stories associated with them. But shifting the traditional tour model to provide extra content, differing perspectives, and distinctive experiences can inject new interest in this program type. The Brigham City Museum of Art and History and Gamble House historic site have found success using a behind-the-scenes approach to these extraexperiential tours with their Behind the Seams and Behind the Velvet Ropes tours, respectively. Both offer different looks at exhibit spaces while allowing audience members closer access and more detailed information than normally available. The Cape Fear Museum's CuraTOURial program also provides detailed, museum-specific information, but it is provided by trained museum curators instead of docents, and the content explores multiple exhibits and collections.

In addition to a glimpse behind the museum curtain, this programming approach can explore new perspectives and provide personal connections to otherwise seemingly unrelatable content. In their Unlocking the Stories program, the Museum of World Treasures uses stories and sensory-based interactives to draw emotional responses from audience members. This approach encourages new understandings and perceptions while allowing participants to personally respond to the museum's interpretation.

LECTURE

Lectures are another common museum program model. Museums explore a variety of topics connected to their missions while allowing audience members the freedom to explore those topics tied to their personal interests. While lectures are often led by field experts, they can be directly tied to and developed around the museum's collection, like the Marshall Steam Museum's Evening at the Museum series, which uses specific objects and collection themes to dictate lecture topics.

Lectures have the expectation of passive, formal instruction for audience consumption, but they can defy this expectation through audience interaction and input. The Jeanerette Museum's History Talks actively encourage audience dialogue and involvement. This practice acknowledges the audience's differing perceptions and individual experiences as it deepens engagement and understanding.

PANEL DISCUSSIONS

Like lectures, panel discussions can explore numerous topics and fields, but rather than sharing a single viewpoint or expert's experience, panels present multiple perceptions and encourage varied discussions. Panel discussions are a great way to explore difficult and adult-themed topics, like the Building Bridges Community Diversity Forum at the Evansville African American Museum. But they can also uncover unique lenses into national and community cultures and history, such as the South County History Center's Palisades Mill: From Wool to Whalers program. Both of these panels bring representatives from different fields, experiences, and understandings to explore a topic of social and historical interest, and each provides new perspectives and encourages dialogue.

SCHEDULED CLASSES

Scheduled classes are a forthright program option for museums. Targeting specific audiences with formal instruction led by topic experts is straightforward and incredibly feasible, regardless of museum size. It provides the opportunity to explore interesting topics in nonmuseum formats, such as the Neon Museum's Hot Yoga class that utilizes outdoor gallery space. It can also provide hands-on instruction for topics that can be beneficial outside the museum environment. Programs like Discovering History through Artifacts at the Bullock Texas State History Museum offer this opportunity to teachers interested in bringing object-based learning into their classrooms. Although these programs utilized the scheduled-class programming model so differently, they are equally successful in advancing their respective missions.

EVENTS

Scheduling events for adult audiences can be equally fun and challenging. To provide the necessary draw and interest, museums should be willing to explore nontraditional museum topics and activities while offering adult perks, such as alcohol, food, and the freedom to express off-color sentiments or responses. To keep these events within the modest resources available, this requires extended cooperation and partnering with community organizations, like breweries, bars, caterers, and adult education institutions. These events can be based on lectures and conversations, like History Happy Hour at the Museum Center at 5ive Points or the Father's Day Beer Talk and Tasting at the Concord Museum, or they can be collections-based conversations centered on peer-to-peer dialogue with museum staff, like the Beer in the Garden event hosted by the Maine Historical Society. These events can even explore adult-centered activities and museum exploration, like the Culture Me Mine Date Night event at the Museum of People and Cultures at Brigham Young University. Regardless, they establish the museum as a comfortable place to have fun and interact with other adult participants, something museums often struggle with creating.

SOCIAL CLUBS

Museums offer a unique chance for adult participants to interact in a themed social environment. In fact, many program participants seek these opportunities precisely for this reason. Some museums are realizing these possibilities and are offering organized social clubs and peer-to-peer interactions through their regularly scheduled programming. These meetings can be formalized around specified activities or topics—the Bonnet Book Club at Cass County's Bonanzaville uses selected books to generate these discussions—or they can be informal conversations based on a chosen theme. The Codington County Heritage Museum and the Marietta Museum of History use this approach with their History Club and Remember When Club meetings, as attendees share thoughts and memories freely during the scheduled time.

SENIOR PROGRAMMING

Programs specifically designed to meet the needs of the aging population fill an often-neglected niche of this adult audience. Senior citizens present their own challenges as a participant base, as cognitive functions, motor skills, and even transportation can present problems. Programs can simply work to help maintain movement and dexterity, like the Tallahassee Museum's Butter Making program. They can offer respite and socialization for both senior participants and their caregivers, such as the History Colorado Center's SPARK! Cultural Programming for People with Memory Loss, or they can help generate cognitive processes and memories, like the Latah County Historical Society's Pastimes and Memories program. This program even travels to nursing and care homes to ensure more participant access. Programs targeting this audience must overcome their own unique set of issues, but they help fulfill the needs of an audience that should never be neglected or forgotten.

MUSEUM SERVICE PROGRAMS

Sometimes, simply offering the museum's expertise can meet a needed programming role. The expertise and experience museum staff can bring to the public are unparalleled, and it can be surprising how much it is desired by a community. The Let's Take a Look program offered by the Museum of Indian Arts and Culture provides curator and collections knowledge to interested visitors. Helping to identify, categorize, and even recommend care options for personal items allows community members to better connect with their personal artifacts while relating to museum objects. Offering this service not only draws people into the museum space, but it also helps ensure the safety of private collections that may one day be donated to the organization.

PROGRAMS FOR ADULTS ONLY

With programs like the Battle of Franklin Trust's Teacher Appreciation Day and the Museum of World Treasures' Unlocking the Stories tour, museums are exploring new ways of attracting adult-only audiences using very little resources. They are offering new opportunities to use their spaces and provide innovative ways to meet adult needs. Even programming for adults with memory loss and their care partners are being explored. To keep adults coming back, museums must draw them through the doors with adult-targeted programming.

Teacher Appreciation Day

Battle of Franklin Trust, Franklin, Tennessee
Historic Sites
Open House
   Target Audience: Local teachers
   Attendance: 50–100 people

Overview: Every year, two historic sites (Carnton House and Carter House) with the Battle of Franklin Trust offer free admission to area teachers when they show their teacher IDs. Teachers can experience sample classroom tours and exhibits to preview what a field trip visit entails, as well as how sites can be incorporated into classroom lessons. They are also offered a discount on educational resources in site gift shops.

Budget: $0

Interpretive Components: ★★★ The purpose of this program is to expose teachers to the resources and experiences available to their classrooms. As such, interpretation is geared toward specific ages and grades, not necessarily to the adult, teacher audience.

Staff Time Requirements: ~8 hours. Teacher Appreciation Day runs during regular open hours, and outside the adjustment for sample tours, it does not require any additional time above the standard workday.

Audience Time Requirements: ~2 hours. The provided sample tours run about an hour for each historic site, but teachers are welcome to spend more time exploring the exhibits and gift shops.

Scalability: ★★★★★ Because this program is run during a regular open day, it can handle as many teachers as the space allows. No additional staff or materials are needed.

Analysis: The Battle of Franklin Trust uses Teacher Appreciation Day components to invite area school personnel to experience for free how these historic sites relate to classroom studies. The open house requires very little museum effort, as it is hosted during regular open hours and the programs previewed are already established within the organization's educational plan. Offering free admission, bookstore discounts, and the opportunity to see what the trust can offer students serves to draw instructors interested in incorporating these options into their lesson plans. The event not only encourages teachers to use the organization's offerings, but it also serves to market these same resources throughout the region's schools in a mutually beneficial format. Any museum that already has tailored educational resources for classroom use or field trip visits could feasibly adapt a similar Teacher Appreciation Day event.

Behind the Seams

Brigham City Museum of Art and History, Brigham City, Utah
History/Art Museum
Tour

Target Audience: Local quilters (adults)

Attendance: 10–25 people

Overview: In association with the annual art quilt exhibition at the museum, the Brigham City Museum of Art and History offers a Behind the Seams tour to give visitors an up-close, thorough look at the details of exhibited pieces. Led by the exhibit curator, staff use white gloves to bring the quilts closer and to show all quilted elements, such as needlework patterns, fabric designs, seam details, and stitch size, to the tour group. Additional information on both individual pieces and the whole exhibit is also shared.

Budget: $0

Interpretive Components: ★★★★ Because it is led by the curator, specific information on each quilt, the artist, and the exhibit can be shared in more detail as participants are given the opportunity to closely examine certain exhibited quilts.

Staff Time Requirements: ~2 hours. In addition to the tour time, preparing selected quilts, gathering necessary materials, and general setup usually takes about an hour.

Audience Time Requirements: ~1 hour. The scheduled tour takes an hour, but questions often take additional time.

Scalability: ★★ Smaller groups allow equal opportunity to examine the pieces as well as encourage questions and discussion. Larger groups greatly diminish this opportunity.

Analysis: Many museum exhibitions attract a professional and hobbyist audience with specific interest in exhibit pieces. Providing the opportunity to better examine these objects with the help of trained museum staff invites this audience into the museum as both students and peers while drawing connections between exhibited pieces and their own perceptions and knowledge. For the Brigham City Museum of Art and History, the Behind the Seams tour offers quilting enthusiasts the chance to examine historic quilts and their artistry within the understanding of their own quilting efforts. Other museums can find similar success using any established collection or exhibit theme. Tours to explore military uniforms or armament, railroad engineering tools, instrument preservation techniques, or even art conservation methods could all translate to this programming model.

Palisades Mill: From Wool to Whalers

South County History Center, South Kingstown, Rhode Island
History Museum
Lecture

Target Audience: Adults

Attendance: 25–50 people

Overview: Palisades Mill: From Wool to Whalers explores the evolving uses and roles of the Palisades Mill historic site. Speakers, including a local historian and the owners of a brewery currently renting the

Figure 4.1 Palisades Mill: From Wool to Whaler's at the South County History Center

space, share varying perspectives on how the site's history and roles have changed over time. Participants are given unique glimpses into the families and businesses associated with the area and are encouraged to explore these community connections within the larger historic narrative.

Budget: $0

Interpretive Components: ★★★★★ Discussions illustrate broad historic and economic concepts through the lens of a single site, including the people associated with it. This allows sweeping interpretive conversations that can be narrowed as needed.

Staff Time Requirements: ~40 hours. This time includes research, speaker recruitment, presentation and program development, marketing, and moderating the panel discussion.

Audience Time Requirements: ~1.5 hours. The panel is scheduled for an hour, with the flexibility to discuss and explore as long as needed.

Scalability: ★★★ The program can accommodate as many people as the space allows, but a small audience may require too much resource delegation per attendee.

Analysis: The Palisades Mill program uses lecture and moderated, panel-like conversations to explore a single historic site's community role from its construction through its contemporary use. This approach helps audience members trace the history of the location and its uses while acknowledging their current experiences with the site. The program expands the traditional historic lecture beyond the past and incorporates modern viewpoints and experiences into the discussion. Numerous historic sites across the country have recently been repurposed and revitalized. Through similar programming efforts, museums can explore these stories to further understand community adaptations and cultural evolution.

Member Preview Day

National Museum of Women in the Arts, Washington, DC
Art Museum
Open House

> **Target Audience:** Museum members
>
> **Attendance:** 100–200 people
>
> **Overview:** When opening new exhibitions, the National Museum of Women in the Arts debuts the space a day early for member-exclusive viewing opportunities. This members-only open house gives attendees special behind-the-scenes access led by curatorial and education staff. Certain exhibitions even include special lectures or artist-led tours. Members also enjoy additional discounts in the museum gift shop and café.
>
> **Budget:** $0
>
> **Interpretive Components:** ★★★★★ The Member Preview Day provides more detailed information than is usually available to the public. The special access allows the audience to explore their interests in new ways.
>
> **Staff Time Requirements:** ~26 hours. The program requires several days' planning as well as three to four people working throughout the event. Cleanup is usually very brief.
>
> **Audience Time Requirements:** Flexible. The event runs for four hours, but members are welcome to come and go as they please. Many members even stay the full time to fully explore the available programs.
>
> **Scalability:** ★★★★★ Because of the open-house nature of the program, only a handful of staff is needed to serve a large audience. If special programming is offered (behind-the-scenes or tours), additional staff may be needed.
>
> **Analysis:** Opening new exhibitions or programs early for a members-only event can doubly benefit a museum. First, it provides an exclusive perk for organization members, inviting their continued support and involvement in museum operations. Adding content through lectures, behind-the-scenes tours, and hands-on programs solidifies the positive experience for the membership audience. Second, it allows the museum to soft-launch the new space. The opportunity to test exhibit components before officially opening to the public is invaluable. The Member Preview program model can easily be adapted for any museum with a membership program willing to dedicate the time.

Let's Take a Look

Museum of Indian Arts and Culture, Santa Fe, New Mexico
Art/History Museum
Open House/Workshop
   Target Audience: Community adults
   Attendance: 10–25 people
   Overview: Once a month, museum curators invite the community to bring in privately owned objects for identification. Not an appraisal system, the program helps connect community members to their personally owned Native American jewelry, pottery, and blankets through museum resources. Object materials, history, purpose, and even artist identification can be explored, as curators examine each piece and then direct visitors to corresponding objects on display in museum galleries.
   Budget: $0
   Interpretive Components: ★★★ While identifying these objects, curators direct program participants to similar objects and their interpretation currently on display throughout the museum. Interested audience members can then observe the similarities between the pieces they own and the pieces in the museum.
   Staff Time Requirements: ~5 hours/month. The two-hour program requires two curators every month. This is in addition to setup and cleanup.
   Audience Time Requirements: ~10 minutes. Program participants can spend as much time in the museum as they like, but time with the curators usually only takes about 10 minutes.
   Scalability: ★★★★★ Once set up, this program works just as well with an audience of 5 as it does for an audience of 100.
   Analysis: The Let's Take a Look program invites community members to take advantage of the museum's expertise. Museums have knowledgeable staff who are experts in their fields. As such, organizations are already seen as objective and final authorities on their collection themes. While some people independently seek a museum's input on private collections, this program model formally invites individuals to utilize a museum's staff. This provides a community service while offering opportunities to interpret care, conservation, and museum best practices in addition to educating participants using displayed objects. Museums willing to facilitate similar conversations can find success through related programming efforts.

History Club

Codington County Heritage Museum, Watertown, South Dakota
History Museum
Social Club
Target Audience: Adults
Attendance: 10–25 people

Credit: Codington County Heritage Museum

Figure 4.2 The History Club at the Codington County Heritage Museum

Overview: History Club is a social gathering of interested adults who meet monthly to share and discuss historic topics of interest. Club members and staff rotate presentation responsibilities and lead a question/ answer or discussion period after. Discussions can cover a variety of subjects, including early county veterinary medicine, US presidential trivia, and videos on national history topics. Presentations take roughly 15 minutes to allow extended conversations and occasional debates.

Budget: $0

Interpretive Components: ★★★ Because presentations are generally very short, the opportunity to share in-depth interpretation is rare. However, the breadth of topics available for discussion ensures every member's interests can be explored.

Staff Time Requirements: ~1.5 hours/month. Time requirements depend on whether staff or volunteers are presenting at that month's meeting. Obviously, staff-led discussions require more staff preparation. When not presenting, staff simply unlock and set up the meeting room.

Audience Time Requirements: ~1 hour. History Club meetings usually run about an hour, depending on member interest in that month's presentation.

Scalability: ★★ This program model can accommodate groups up to about 30 attendees. After that point, adjustments must be made for time and discussion, as small-group breakouts would become necessary rather than a round-table discussion.

Analysis: The understanding that museums can provide social opportunities is a relatively new one, and while other organizations are exploring more formalized and complex collaboration opportunities, Codington County's History Club takes a straightforward approach that requires minimal staff maintenance. At its foundation, it simply requires a group of interested people and a space to meet. Staff can allow club members to take as little or as much responsibility for meeting presentations as they like, and topics can be selected using member interest and the museum mission. History, art, and science can be equally viable for club presentations. Other museums interested in exploring social clubs have the freedom to form the club however best fits their resources and abilities.

Evening at the Museum

Marshall Steam Museum, Yorklyn, Delaware
History Museum
Lecture

Target Audience: Adults

Attendance: 25–50 people

Overview: Evening at the Museum includes evening lectures that invite guest speakers and audience members to explore the museum's collection, behind-the-scenes topics, and community history. Each themed lecture covers different topics and objects, both historic and contemporary, allowing attendees a closer interaction with the museum collection. Past subjects include historic sites and their connection to the community, local family businesses stretching over multiple generations, the museum's famed steam car collection, and recent historic research concerning museum themes and collections.

Budget: $0

Interpretive Components: ★★★★★ Topics and speakers are selected to explore the breadth of the museum's collection as well as its connection to local history. This allows the series to appeal to a wider audience. Guest speakers are chosen for their expertise and ability to share their knowledge.

Evening at the Museum event at the Marshall Steam Museum

Staff Time Requirements: ~18 hours. Education staff not only select the topics and research and recruit the speaker-volunteers, but they also set up and clean up for the event. This includes collecting event evaluations.

Audience Time Requirements: ~1 hour. Lectures are designed to run about 45 minutes, but question-and-answer times often run over.

Scalability: ★★★★ This event can easily accommodate as few or as many people as the space and staff can manage.

Analysis: The Marshall Steam Museum uses the Evening at the Museum model to establish consistent and varied discussions that explore the depth and far-reaching effects of their collection. Even using multiple presentation types (e.g., lecture, tour, discussion, etc.) ensures that each program is different, attracting a distinctive audience and expanding the museum's reach. While dedication to this variability requires significant time and energy to plan the events, find qualified volunteer-speakers, and create appropriate programming environments, it can result in regular programming success and foster new audience support and partnerships. Museums willing to commit this time can achieve similar relationships.

CuraTOURial

Cape Fear Museum, Wilmington, North Carolina
History/Science Museum
Tour

Target Audience: Adults

Attendance: 10–25 people

Overview: CuraTOURial is a special tour led by curatorial staff that provides an in-depth look at the museum, its history, and its collections. The tour includes a multimedia presentation about the museum's background and mission, as well as discussions about specific artifacts and an exploration of museum galleries and exhibitions. Because each group is led by museum curators, interpretation can include a more in-depth discussion about museums, their role, and the objects and exhibits currently on display. This provides a deeper experience for those taking the tour.

Budget: $0

Interpretive Components: ★★★★ This tour provides detailed information not available during a normal visit and allows participants to explore the museum from a curatorial perspective.

Staff Time Requirements: 2 hours. In addition to leading the tour, staff must develop the multimedia presentation as well as select the objects to be discussed.

Audience Time Requirements: 1 hour. The CuraTOURial program takes an hour to complete.

Scalability: ★★ This tour works best with a smaller number of people. Larger audiences would need to split, requiring more staff to lead the extra groups.

Analysis: While many museums offer behind-the-scenes programming, specifically using curatorial staff is less common. Making curators available for this program not only gives tour participants a new perspective on museum displays, but also the curator-led groups receive additional information not normally available to general visitors. The CuraTOURial program goes a step farther by using the tour as an opportunity to explore the Cape Fear Museum, its exhibit process, and its role in the community. This expanded interpretation connects museum operations with mission responsibilities and encourages deeper comprehension. While some museum curators may be unwilling to lead this type of tour, museums willing to offer direct curator–visitor interpretation can broaden visitor understandings and, through them, garner additional community support.

Bonnet Book Club

Cass County Historical Society–Bonanzaville, West Fargo, North Dakota
History Museum
Social Club

Target Audience: Retired adults

Attendance: Less than 10 people

Overview: The Bonnet Book Club allows local retirees to gather at the museum to discuss a selected book. Led by a volunteer, the club meets every other month and chooses books related to the museum mission, including topics concerning pioneers, homesteads, and regional history. Club meetings can also include special presentations and site tours relevant to that month's book. Museum–club partnerships even extend to the giftshop, as the bookstore will include selected books for members to purchase.

Budget: $0

Interpretive Components: ★★ All interpretive information is provided through the selected reading. Fiction, nonfiction, and books that explore historic themes can be included, but it can be difficult to manage the historic accuracy included in the reading material.

Staff Time Requirements: ~1 hour. Because the club is led by a volunteer, staff responsibilities are limited to preparing and cleaning up the space for the meeting.

Audience Time Requirements: ~4 hours. Club members read the book at their leisure and then gather for an hour-and-a-half discussion.

Scalability: ★★★★ The Bonnet Cook Club can work easily for just a handful of people, or it can be adjusted for up to 50 members. Larger groups would require small discussion groups to be organized.

Analysis: Gathering to discuss views and perceptions of a common book allows participants to gather socially in a semiorganized environment while exploring differing viewpoints and projections. For a museum, hosting book groups like this not only provides a community service, but it also offers the opportunity to explore collection themes in a nonthreatening, open way. As such, this programming model could allow varying amounts of staff involvement—from a complete hands-off approach like the Bonnet Book Club to staff planning all meeting discussion components—and could potentially work for any museum type.

Discovering History through Artifacts

Bullock Texas State History Museum, Austin, Texas
History Museum
Workshop

Target Audience: Local teachers

Attendance: 10–25 people

Overview: Using interaction with historic objects, Discovering History through Artifacts instructs community teachers how to use artifacts in their classrooms to excite and engage students. Participants learn artifact analysis skills and step-by-step teaching techniques to practice identifying "mystery objects" and how these methods can enhance classroom les-

Credit: Bullock
Texas State History
Museum

*Figure 4.4 Discovery History through Artifacts at the
Bullock Texas State History Museum*

sons. Participants are then free to explore museum exhibitions to exercise these skills and find connections to historic and other curricular topics.

Budget: $0

Interpretive Components: ★★★★ This workshop uses a multidisciplinary approach to tie the artifacts to art, science, math, and social studies while instructing participants in real-world methods to incorporate learned skills into school studies.

Staff Time Requirements: 4 hours. Once developed, this workshop requires about four hours: one hour of prep time and three to run the event.

Audience Time Requirements: 3 hours. Discovering History through Artifacts is split into several sections to break up the three-hour run time. An hour and a half is spent learning about artifact analysis. An hour is given to explore the museum, and the final 30 minutes are spent discussing the process and sharing observations.

Scalability: ★★★★ This program workshop is limited by the instruction space available and the number of artifacts on hand. Smaller groups allow each participant to work individually with the artifacts, while larger groups could be split into smaller units to share the artifacts.

Analysis: The ability to use artifact analysis in the classroom benefits teachers and museums alike. Recent recognition of the value of object-based learning in enhancing student meaning making and long-term retention is leading teachers to seek professional-development opportunities to expand their use of these methodologies in their own lesson plans. Having practiced these skills for years, museums like the Bullock Texas State History Museum are in the ideal position to provide this education. Taking the time to share these techniques with local teachers only requires a small hands-on collection and the instruction space. If the museum takes additional measures to qualify this instruction as part of state-mandated professional development, then its value to teachers is ensured.

Beer in the Garden

Maine Historical Society, Portland, Maine
History Museum
Open House
  Target Audience: Adults
  Attendance: 50–100 people
  Overview: Beer in the Garden is a monthly evening event where selected objects are displayed to spark informal discussions with museum curators. Complimentary beer donated by local breweries and snacks are made available in the museum garden as audience members are free to socialize and discuss that night's event themes. The open house often features special speakers, live music, and even a fire pit. Past topics include the history of music in Maine, traditional toys and games, and historic foodways.
  Budget: $0
  Interpretive Components: ★★ Each informal meeting uses selected museum objects to inspire discussion. Conversation depth and length depends on audience interest.
  Staff Time Requirements: ~21 hours/program. The event requires five or six staff members over the course of the event for setup, facilitation, and cleanup. In addition, the curator can spend several hours selecting themed objects for the event.
  Audience Time Requirements: Flexible. The event runs two hours every month, but audience members have complete flexibility for how long they stay.
  Scalability: ★★★ The biggest challenges in scaling this event is how much space and the amount of donated alcohol is available. While donated drinks can be offered until they're gone, running out too early in the event can result in negative audience reactions and limit attendance for subsequent events.
  Analysis: Beer in the Garden is an adult happy hour hosted at the museum with the hope of sparking museum-themed conversations.

Offering free drinks and snacks attracts an audience, while a variety of themed objects encourages semimoderated conversations where attendees can socialize with peers. Topics can be flexible, and interpretation can be as detailed as individual visitors desire. While keeping this event under a consistent resource cap (e.g., less than $100) is heavily dependent on the willingness of local breweries, bars, or alcohol supply companies, these relationships can be nurtured through mutually beneficial partnerships. For example, by providing the needed beverages, a business can be listed as an event sponsor. Museums willing to develop these needed relationships should be able to tailor a similar event to their mission.

Pastimes and Memories

Latah County Historical Society, Moscow, Idaho
History Museum
Offsite
Oral History/Partnership
   Target Audience: Residents at local assisted-living communities
   Attendance: 10–25 people
   Overview: In partnership with the local public library and the assisted-living community, the Latah County Historical Society coordinates a monthly, off-site program. Using hands-on museum artifacts and historic photographs, assisted-living residents are encouraged to share their thoughts and memories of the community. Discussions stimulate memory recall and peer-to-peer interactions while allowing the museum to connect with the residents and possibly add to their archival records. In addition, the public library provides a reading list related to program themes for resident use.
   Budget: $0
   Interpretive Components: ★★ While program staff include information on the objects and photos provided, the purpose of the program is to inspire participants to share their own recollections and interpretation among themselves and with attending staff.
   Staff Time Requirements: ~3 hours. The program takes one to two hours of preparation, with the program running an hour.
   Audience Time Requirements: Flexible. Museum staff provide objects and photographs on-site for about an hour, but resident participants can come and go as their interests dictate.
   Scalability: ★★★★★ This program can work for one to two people or for the entire assisted-living community, provided enough objects and photographs can be passed around.
   Analysis: Using museum education collections to stimulate memories and discussions among older audience members provides them the

opportunity to reminisce and share personal experiences with their peers, resident staff, and museum representatives. This not only strengthens cognitive functions and improves communication skills, but it also has the added benefit of improving overall quality of life within the facility. While Pastimes and Memories is specifically oriented to historic objects and photographs, related programs using art, environment, and occupational tools could be adapted for other museum organizations.

Behind the Velvet Ropes

Gamble House, Pasadena, California
Historic Site
Tour
   Target Audience: Adults
   Attendance: Less than 10 people

Photograph courtesy of The Gamble House, USC, ©Alexander Vertikoff / Vertikoff Archive

Figure 4.5 Interior, Gamble House. Image from the publication "The Gamble House: Building Paradise in California"

Overview: Behind the Velvet Ropes allows participants to see spaces and details not available during normal tours. Equipped with flashlights and white gloves, experienced docents take the opportunity to share behind-the-scenes information through their own passion and knowledge of the historic site. Light refreshments are included.

Budget: $45

Interpretive Components: ★★★★★ This program allows participants to explore the historic site in more detail than the public is usually allowed. Back rooms, closed drawers, and unopened closets are revealed, and docents include their individual stories and interpretations not included in scripted tours.

Staff Time Requirements: 3 hours. The program requires a single staff person to facilitate each tour group.

Audience Time Requirements: 2.5 hours. Behind the Velvet Ropes tours run two and a half hours to showcase those spaces not included on a standard tour.

Scalability: ★★ This tour can only be managed with very small groups. Larger groups not only do not fit in the historic rooms, but they also are unable to explore the detailed pieces.

Analysis: Behind the Velvet Ropes allows visitors to satisfy their curiosity—under supervision, of course—by exploring the hidden details of the Gamble House's architecture, furniture, and exhibit areas. These features are not accessible during normal visiting opportunities, so the program removes the barriers (both physical and metaphorical), and tour participants are able to fully experience the space: unlocking closets, investigating nooks, and opening drawers. In addition to guiding the audience through this exploration, guides are given additional freedom to share stories and facts not part of the regular, scripted interpretation. This opens the museum to visitors in new and exciting ways, as they are given access beyond traditional "this is what it looks like, this is what we do" behind-the-scenes programs. While allowing such access can be frightening to museum staff, specifically guiding the visitors' experience can open these spaces without endangering the collection while providing exclusive and memorable visitor encounters.

Butter Making

Tallahassee Museum, Tallahassee, Florida
History/Science Museum
Workshop

  Target Audience: Senior citizens
  Attendance: 10–25 people

Overview: Butter Making explores the history, benefits, and uses of butter using a "churn as you learn" approach. Designed for senior audiences, the workshop looks at various processes for making the product while using fine motor skills and encouraging memory. Multiple processes are explored as participants create their own butter sample. Each participant can take this sample home after the workshop.

Budget: $50

Interpretive Components: ★★★★ Not only does the workshop cover how to make butter, but it also explores the history and benefits of the material. Creative butter uses are also discussed during the churning process. This is in addition to the skills and cognitive components specifically designed for senior audiences.

Staff Time Requirements: ~1.5 hours. Staff time includes food preparation, setup, and cleanup. It does not include program planning.

Audience Time Requirements: ~1 hour. The workshop runs about 45 minutes in addition to question-and-answer times.

Scalability: ★★ This program works best with smaller audiences. Larger groups require additional resources and make instruction more difficult. It really cannot handle more than about 25 people at a time.

Analysis: Butter Making uses an activity-based program method to meet specific skills and cognitive needs of the senior audience. On the surface, this workshop looks very much like it would appeal to a variety of audiences, but because the Tallahassee Museum specifically targets senior audiences, they are able to focus on building identified abilities through discussions and hands-on components. This program emphasis helps to create a safe, welcoming environment for seniors to work with these skills while exploring varying perspectives of a well-known material. Programs targeting this audience would benefit by tying audience skills maintenance to unrelated program interpretation.

Hot Yoga

Neon Museum, Las Vegas, Nevada
History / Art Museum
In-Gallery / Partnership
  Target Audience: Adults
  Attendance: 10–25 people
  Overview: Hot Yoga is a one-hour yoga class taught by a certified instructor at the Neon Museum. Capitalizing on the heat of the desert climate, the class takes place in the museum's outdoor exhibit area, called the Boneyard. Because the museum is only available to the public via a scheduled tour, Hot Yoga allows participants to experience the museum on their schedule without having to take the formal tour.
  Budget: $50
  Interpretive Components: ★ Although the yoga class takes place in an outdoor exhibit area, there is no specific focus on art interpretation.
  Staff Time Requirements: 10 hours. Staff time includes setup and cleanup for each one-hour class. Each schedule rotation includes four classes.

Audience Time Requirements: 1 hour. Hot Yoga classes run for one hour.

Scalability: ★★★ Class size is limited by the exhibit space it uses and the minimum number of participants the instructor is willing to teach.

Analysis: Hot Yoga allows participants to experience the museum environment using a decidedly nonmuseum programming model. The museum–instructor partnership offers clean, open space for the class while exposing attendees to the collection and exhibit spaces. It presents the chance to experience the museum in new and different contexts while solidifying community relationships and building support. Museums willing to work with instructors can find their galleries opened for any variety of activities for which museum staff have little planning or facilitation responsibilities. This offers creative programming solutions without depleting museum resources.

Building Bridges Community Diversity Forum

Evansville African American Museum, Evansville, Indiana
History/Culture Museum
Lecture/Workshop

Target Audience: Community residents (adults)

Attendance: 100–200 people

Overview: The Building Bridges Community Diversity Forum invites community residents to share varying experiences and issues related to diversity, culture, discrimination, and inclusion. One part lecture or panel discussion, one part open discussion and interaction, the program encourages participants to discuss ways to promote changes and to share steps to combat social issues on a local level. The museum provides context and a safe space to explore these difficult and sometimes-controversial issues. The goal is to build understanding on the importance of diversity.

Budget: $50

Interpretive Components: ★★★★ Open-forum discussions encourage participation on a personal and relevant level in relation to discrimination, diversity, and inclusion. The Evansville African American Museum's program explores these difficult topics through the lens of African American history and culture while exploring ways to effect change within the local community.

Staff Time Requirements: ~1.5 hours. Time includes setup, facilitating the event, and cleanup. It does not include planning and event coordination.

Audience Time Requirements: 1 hour. The Building Bridges Community Diversity Forum runs for one hour. This includes both the panel discussion and audience input.

Scalability: ★★★★ A forum-style program can accommodate any scale audience. Smaller groups can encourage more intimate discussion and personal sharing. Larger groups can provide wider experiences but will often require a sound system.

Analysis: The Building Bridges Community Diversity Forum provides an open environment to explore the challenging topic of diversity and inclusion. The program offers audience members the chance to hear multiple perspectives while presenting the opportunity to share their own thoughts and experiences in a safe, nonthreatening space. This open, discussion-based program moves beyond simply sharing thoughts and opinions and purposefully moves into actionable goals that can be achieved on the local level. This program model has huge potential to affect museum social goals, but it is not an easy one to duplicate. Perhaps the greatest challenge in duplicating this program is staff willingness to tackle the difficult and perceived controversy of these topics. Special training and staff preparation may be necessary to manage a similar successful event.

Remember When Club

Marietta Museum of History, Marietta, Georgia
History Museum
Oral History/Social Club
   Target Audience: Adults
   Attendance: More than 200 people
   Overview: The Remember When Club is an oral history organization that meets monthly to discuss various historic topics and share specific memories. Often using both speaker and panel formats to help focus stories and experiences, audience members are encouraged to join in the discussion. Past topics include county higher education, public housing, veteran stories, and historic community events. Meetings are recorded and added to the museum's oral history archive.
   Budget: $50
   Interpretive Components: ★★★ Topics vary by subject, audience, and place. Themes, including restaurants, shopping, and major local events, must directly relate to Cobb County history, its businesses, and its people. Club members and other audience attendees provide the context and interpretation by sharing their personal memories.
   Staff Time Requirements: ~8 hours. Club meetings require some initial planning to decide topics and invite panelists, among other things. However, once set, meetings require little time. For each event, staff set up the space, introduce the panelists, run the recording equipment, and clean up.

Audience Time Requirements: ~1.5 hours. Each meeting runs about an hour and a half. This includes panelist discussions and audience contributions.

Scalability: ★★★★★ The Remember When Club can be run for a handful of people, or it can be adapted to encompass an entire auditorium.

Analysis: While the Remember When Club offers a fun, social gathering for club members, it greatly benefits the Marietta Museum of History's archival collection. Using consistent, directed discussions among a dedicated older group allows the museum regular oral history information to improve their archive collection. Keeping meeting themes focused further deepens museum understanding and improves their research capabilities. Many museums struggle with stagnating archival collections, whether through the lack of new donations or the absence of multiple historic perspectives, and such programs as the Remember When Club offer the opportunity to continuously revisit historic events, organizations, and characters through new viewpoints. Museums interested in finding similar content to supplement their collection can explore unlimited topics, including historic events, differing scientific viewpoints, and even artists' historic contexts.

SPARK! Cultural Programming for People with Memory Loss

History Colorado Center, Denver, Colorado
History Museum
Partnership/Workshop

Target Audience: Adults with memory loss and their caregivers

Attendance: 10–25 people

Overview: History Colorado Center's SPARK! program partners with the Alzheimer's Association and other Denver museums to provide tailored programs for individuals with early to midstage memory loss and their care partners. Participants are able to enjoy museum galleries and related interactive and multisensory activities in a safe and welcoming environment that encourages social interaction while building and maintaining cognitive abilities. Programs have included guest speakers, activity-based learning, and exhibit demonstrations.

Budget: $50

Interpretive Components: ★★★★★ Each program focuses on a different museum gallery space, pairing it with a related activity or discussion intended to engage participants with memory loss. Activities like photo sharing and small group discussions are designed to meet the specific needs and abilities of this audience.

Figure 4.6 SPARK! Cultural Programming for People with Memory Loss at the History Colorado Center

Staff Time Requirements: ~4 hours/program. Staff plan, test, and facilitate each program, in addition to handling registration, setting up, and cleaning up afterward.

Audience Time Requirements: ~1.5 hours. Programs run a little over an hour, with additional time to complete activities, ask questions, or further explore the chosen exhibit.

Scalability: ★★ This program works best with a smaller audience to ensure a low facilitator-to-participant ratio. Smaller groups not only encourage more engagement but also help maintain individual well-being.

Analysis: The SPARK! program uses museum spaces to facilitate learning and social interaction while fostering cognitive and occupational therapies for attendees with dementia and memory loss. Interpretation is often considered secondary to building and maintaining these abilities. The program additionally provides opportunities for caretakers to experience museum offerings without the added stress of managing their dementia partners. In this way, the museum is able to provide a specific service to an often-ignored or grossly underserved community audience. Dementia-based programming can be adapted for any museum organization, including art, science, history, or technology. However, staff working with this audience would benefit from additional training to ensure participant safety and well-being.

History Talks

Jeanerette Museum, Jeanerette, Louisiana
Historic Site/History Museum
Lecture
   Target Audience: Adults (only)
   Attendance: 50–100 people
   Overview: Twice a year, the Jeanerette Museum hosts free history-themed talks. Drawing from both local and statewide history, events may incorporate film viewings, professor-led discussions, author presentations, or even music. The program attracts both rural and urban audiences and encourages participants to contribute through dialogue, submitting photographs, or sharing family stories. The diverse audience and varied topics ensure each talk is unique.
   Budget: $60
   Interpretive Components: ★★★ Each History Talk is usually led by an acknowledged expert, but audience members are often encouraged to share their own experiences to help expand the topic under discussion.
   Staff Time Requirements: ~4 hours/program. Staff and volunteers coordinate the talks, establish program logistics, and manage setting up and cleaning up the space.
   Audience Time Requirements: ~1.5 hours. Talk length may vary depending on topic and speaker, but they rarely exceed an hour and a half.
   Scalability: ★★★★ Depending on space and audiovisual needs, the History Talks program can equally serve small groups or an audience of several hundred.
   Analysis: The Jeanerette Museum's History Talks differ from traditional lecture-based programming by encouraging extended audience interaction. Each discussion is expert led, but audience-provided perspectives and information equally direct the program's agenda while enhancing the program's interpretive reach. Many programs even go so far as to request audience-submitted content (e.g., photographs, stories, etc.) prior to the event so they can be incorporated into planned event components. While many museums have found success in the traditional lecture-focused program talk, audiences are looking for ways to add their stories to larger narratives and to help add relevance to their programming experience. Shifting this program method to not only include but also depend on audience participation requires a commitment from both museum staff and any outside presenters.

Culture Me Mine Date Night

Museum of People and Cultures at Brigham Young University, Provo, Utah
History/Culture Museum
Event
   Target Audience: Adult couples
   Attendance: 10–25 people
   Overview: Designed to provide a unique date-night experience, Culture Me Mine Date Night invites couples to explore the museum through several partially guided experiences. Starting with a team scavenger hunt, couples explore the museum, searching for specific objects or information. Once all participants have arrived and had a chance for this brief self-exploration, attendees are led on a guided tour through museum galleries, including temporary exhibit spaces. Couples are then split and matched against their partners for a spirited game of "Couples Feud" as they answer questions about the museum, exhibits, and university. The event concludes with gallery-themed craft activities, such as creating unique pottery and receiving awards like "most authentic" and "most creative."
   Budget: $75
   Interpretive Components: ★★★★★ Event participants are encouraged to interact with the museum through a variety of ways, including self-exploration, guided tours, and hands-on activities. This variety satisfies multiple learning styles and interests to ensure that each participant is engaged and enjoys their time.
   Staff Time Requirements: ~12 hours. Time includes preparation, setup, cleanup, and conducting the event.
   Audience Time Requirements: 1.5 hours. The event runs for about an hour and a half as couples explore the museum, participate in the guided components, and enjoy refreshments.
   Scalability: ★★★ This event depends on an intimate and personal environment. Larger audiences make maintaining this environment difficult.
   Analysis: The Culture Me Mine Date Night event uses museum spaces to encourage couples' engagement and friendly competition. Attendees are free to experience the museum using both traditional and nontraditional methods while interacting with social peers and the museum's collection. The adult environment embraces fun engagement while targeting adult themes and interpretive opportunities. This allows audience members a unique museum experience while breaking down many of the perceived barriers in visiting the museum (e.g., child-only programming, boring conversations, no social collaboration, etc.). Because of the program's focus on providing a fun, entertaining couples event, similar programming efforts can be duplicated at any museum.

Unlocking the Stories

Museum of World Treasures, Wichita, Kansas
History / Art Museum
Tour / Partnership
  Target Audience: Adults
  Attendance: 25–50 people

Figure 4.7 Unlocking the Stories tour participants at the Museum of World Treasures

Overview: Unlocking the Stories is an immersive, experience-based tour that uses stories to explore specific artifacts in both gallery exhibits and the staff-only curatorial area. The tour includes a guided program through museum galleries, a curatorial workshop, and a hands-on artifact activity where participants are encouraged to use their smartphones to investigate the object's purpose. Tours are explicitly designed to open audience members to the emotions in each story while connecting those emotional responses to their own experiences. The tour allows these emotions to be explored and analyzed in a safe and encouraging environment.
  Budget: $75
Interpretive Components: ★★★★★ Detailed stories paired with the opportunity for individual observation allows participants to relate to the artifact(s) of their choice. This approach ensures audience engagement and memories of the program long after it finishes.

Staff Time Requirements: 200 hours. Because of its emotional foundation, this program saw intensive preparation, evaluation, and testing before it was made publicly available. Representatives from the local tourism bureau and a professional consultant worked closely in developing and marketing the tour. Now fully developed, each tour requires approximately two hours' staff time.

Audience Time Requirements: 2 hours. The full program takes two hours to complete the tour, workshop, and activity components.

Scalability: ★★ Technically, the tour can be conducted for a single person. However, groups should not be more than 50 people to ensure engagement and participation standards.

Analysis: Unlocking the Stories seeks to provide participants the opportunity to emotionally connect with not only the museum's collection but also the individuals associated with each piece. This emotional response encourages deeper understandings, as emotion makes memory and thus ensures an unforgettable experience. While museums regularly work to document and connect objects with stories, finding opportunities for visitors to not only hear these stories but also expressively associate with them can be more difficult and even uncomfortable. Museums interested in fostering similar audience-centered programming may need to explore additional training for program guides.

Father's Day Beer Talk and Tasting

Concord Museum, Concord, Massachusetts
History Museum
Event/Partnership
    Target Audience: Fathers and adult children
    Attendance: 25–50 people
    Overview: For Father's Day, the Concord Museum partnered with the Rapscallion Brewery of Acton to host a talk and beer tasting at the Wright Tavern historic site. While staff led a discussion on the material culture and importance of Revolutionary beer at the museum, the brewery provided the tasting component at the tavern, where audience members could explore a site not normally open to the public.
    Budget: $100
    Interpretive Components: ★★★★ The discussion portion of the event included both the cultural importance of beer and alcohol in the 18th century and the importance of the Wright Tavern in local Revolutionary era history. This paired the broader 18th-century cultural discussion with a focus on a local historic site.

Figure 4.8 Attendees at the Concord Museum's Beer History Talk and Tasting have a taste of Rapscallion Beer at historic Wright Tavern in Concord, MA.

Staff Time Requirements: ~8 hours. Staff spent roughly six hours coordinating and researching for the event. Event setup and cleanup added an additional two hours.

Audience Time Requirements: 2 hours. Time at the Concord Museum for the talk and exhibit exploration filled the first hour, with the audience free to spend the final hour exploring the brewery's selection and the historic site.

Scalability: ★★ This event was heavily dependent on space availability. While a smaller audience would be easier, it is less cost effective.

Scaling up would require more space and the possibility of involving additional breweries.

Analysis: The Father's Day Beer Talk and Tasting paired a traditional lecture-based program with alcohol and the opportunity to explore a privately held historic site. The museum–brewery partnership opened numerous opportunities to share event responsibilities while expanding each organization's audience reach. The museum provided historical context on the brewery business and the tavern site, while the brewery used their serving license to share their product. Each organization used their own marketing list, drawing two seemingly dissimilar groups together to share the experience. This partnership was vital to the event's success and must be considered fundamental for any museum interested in duplicating the program.

History Happy Hour

Museum Center at 5ive Points, Cleveland, Tennessee
History Museum
Event/Partnership
    Target Audience: Adults (only)
    Attendance: 25–50 people
    Overview: Five times throughout the year, the Museum Center at 5ive Points hosts a History Happy Hour, where museum staff present a selected local history topic while enjoying a free beer bar and refreshments. Partnering with a local brewery and financial sponsor, the museum is able to offer adult beverages while exploring local history and demonstrating objects associated with it. Guest speakers, selected collection objects, and live music have all been used.
    Budget: $100
    Interpretive Components: ★★★ Museum representatives interpret museum exhibits and objects while offering a hands-on, demonstration component. Information and activities change based on the event's theme.
    Staff Time Requirements: 8 hours/event. This includes planning, coordinating, and manning the event.
    Audience Time Requirements: 2 hours. History Happy Hour runs for two hours to allow audience members time to socialize, explore the themed interpretation, and enjoy the refreshments.
    Scalability: ★★★ Smaller audiences are always easier to manage, while larger audiences make activities and engagement more difficult. Still, larger groups could be managed using more lecture-style interpretation or by creating a more regimented schedule rotation.
    Analysis: The Museum Center at 5ive Points fosters a dedicated History Happy Hour audience by regularly scheduling programs

Credit: Museum Center at 5ive Points

*Figure 4.9 History Happy Hour: Cherokee at the Museum Center
at 5ive Points*

with different presentation themes. This variety encourages repeat participants, as each event offers a different topic and perspective while providing a comfortable, social space with adult refreshments. This consistency
requires significant dedication by museum staff to develop each program,
network and nurture the required community partnerships, and man the
events. Museums willing to take the time to foster and maintain such
networks could feasibly duplicate a similar event.

5

Programming for Multigenerational Audiences

When describing the most common museum visitor group, regardless of museum location or type, one can expect the answer to include children, adults, retirees, and the occasional teen. While individually these audiences deserve programming uniquely suited to their needs, there is something to be said for museum programs that actively seek to target them collectively.

It can be difficult to engage a group of such wide age ranges, experiences, and expectations, but that doesn't eliminate the need to try. Multigenerational groups require programs that meet the needs of each generation it includes in addition to group-specific expectations for their visit. At the least, these audiences look for audience-driven content where they control the flow of information and can take part in intimate conversations that bring their group into a deeper relationship with the museum and with each other. They want their experience to be personal, and they want the flexibility to do it on their terms.

To appeal to these multigenerational groups, museums must learn to combine different program components to create a blended museum experience. Staff must allow this audience to contribute to their visit by sharing personal experiences and expectations. Museums must grow comfortable with in-depth, sometimes-uncomfortable discussions, and they must work with the visitors' need to explore museum content on their own pace and schedule. Successfully engaging this audience requires flexibility, variety, and a willingness to relinquish program control.

WORKSHOPS

For many museums, workshops fill a challenging programming niche. These scheduled classes focus on hands-on and guided instruction by a field expert and can cover an unlimited number of fields, topics, and processes. Everything from the German American Heritage Center's How to Make Sauerkraut workshop to the History Colorado Center's Historical Craft Society follows this program model while encouraging social collaboration as participants are able to blend their experiences for better understandings.

TOURS

Tours are a familiar and comfortable program for most museums, but to adequately reach a multigenerational audience and meet their needs, these tours should be expanded to include unique experiences and content not available to the general museum visitor. For the Mai Wah Society's Below the Scenes tour, this includes exploring staff-only areas of the museum while hearing behind-the-scenes information. For the Conrad-Caldwell House Museum's Twilight Tours and the Lahaina Restoration Foundation's Baldwin Home Candlelight Tour, this means exploring after hours using alternative lighting (e.g., flashlights and candles) to provide new perspectives on historic spaces.

Changing the traditional tour model can even mean shifting the tour's location and interpretive approach. The Johnson County Jim Gatchell Memorial Museum's Echoes of the Past Cemetery Tours and the Grout Museum District's Strolling with the Spirits program have addressed this by leading their tours through the local cemeteries, where audience members meet costumed actors portraying specific historic characters. They even explore program scheduling by offering these tours during expected holiday times (former) and coordinated with major anniversaries, both local and national (latter).

EVENTS

Major museum events are a recognizable component of museum program plans, but they can be time consuming and resource draining. For these reasons, they are often given a limited schedule. Annual or even semiannual events require large planning commitments; logistical challenges for space and audience size; and unique coordination with volunteers, outside experts, and other partnering organizations.

Event programming can be as varied as the museum's collection. They can utilize public-domain materials, like the Museum Center at 5ive Points' *Sergeant York* Film Viewing. They can encourage community input and participation, such as the Blanden Art Museum's Poetry N' Rhythm.

They can even explore difficult social issues, like the Moody Museum's Panel Discussion on Race and Ethnicity. These events required time to organize, plan, network, and manage, but they also use unique interpretive approaches to attract multiple generational audience members.

DEMONSTRATIONS

Demonstrations offer brief, interactive snippets of interpretation from field experts to engage audience members. Because demonstrations tend to be directed toward smaller groups, opportunities are available to discuss and adjust material to fit the audience's ages, abilities, and interests. The Amherst Historical Society's Flax: From Plant to Thread brings the historic process discussed in its exhibits into the hands of a visiting artisan. For the Indiana State Museum and Historic Sites' Museum Collection Protection: Gallery Cleaning, it illustrates proper museum cleaning practices and offers explanations for special processes and methods. Both show visitors the intricate steps involved with that specific task without taking the time to detail and teach the method.

OUTDOOR PROGRAM PARTNERSHIPS

Using outdoor programming as opportunities to explore community partnerships can be a great way to expand a museum's recognition and reach in its community. While it requires time to nurture needed relationships and plan the program, it can draw new audiences and encourage new engagement strategies. Both the Grout Museum District and the Neon Museum use this model to explore after-hours astronomy through their Star Parties and Stars and Stardust: Sidewalk Astronomy in the Neon Boneyard programs, respectively. Each partner with local astronomy organizations to provide telescopes for their programs. While Star Parties is offered on a regular basis, Stars and Stardust takes the opportunity to incorporate additional star-themed interpretation and activities. Both use their space and community organizations wisely while effecting different programmatic activities to appeal to a slightly different audience type.

COMMUNITY EXHIBITS

Community exhibits are a great way to create audience-driven content through museum-oriented exhibits. Museums can display community-created collections, driving personally relevant exhibits and encouraging multigenerational collaboration. These exhibits can be a small display from a single contributor, like the Alutiiq Museum and Archaeology Repository's Meet the Artist program. It can be a formally planned and curated exhibit, like the Haines Sheldon Museum's Six-Week Spotlight, or it can be a special themed, event-specific space, such as the Moody Museum's Veteran's Day Program. Each uses themes and content provided by the community but managed and displayed through the museums' gallery spaces.

WALK-UP PROGRAMS

Many multigenerational groups seek museum experiences that they can explore at their own pace, molding the museum to their needs and expectations. Programs that offer a walk-in or walk-up option appeal because they permit this audience to engage with what attracts their curiosity and allow them to work within the interests and perceptions of the group. This can take the shape of simple touch carts, like the Hands-On History Carts provided by the Oklahoma History Center, or it can be slightly more formal through brief, semiguided docent conversations, like the Shelburne Museum's 1 in 10 program. It can even be station-oriented activities or a planned open house, like the Kenosha Public Museum's Women in Science Fair. These programs require the museum to relinquish group movement and attention back to the audience.

COMMUNITY OUTREACH

Community outreach programs pull museum content outside the museum's walls and into community spaces. This often requires dedicated partnerships between local organizations, businesses, and individuals for success. The Tread of Pioneers Museum's Yule Log Hunt illustrates this need, as the museum works with the local newspapers, radio stations, and community businesses to blend local history with a holiday scavenger hunt for donated prizes. In fact, for this particular program, participants may never actually enter the museum's grounds, but they can't help but be involved in the museum's mission as they research and solve the necessary riddles to find the yule log.

PODCASTS

Podcasts are a digital medium not often utilized by museums but one that reaches numerous audience members. Like the Snapchat or Tumblr accounts from chapter 3, they have the potential to reach a large, international audience at the listeners' convenience, but unlike those social media platforms, podcasts do not encourage active conversation with subscribers. This means the museum maintains control over the content, length, and depth of the interpretation provided. Listeners choose which recordings catch their interests and when they wish to listen.

PROGRAMS FOR MULTIGENERATIONAL AUDIENCES

Multigenerational groups are daily occurrences in the museum field, and museums must learn to reach all members while remaining within the limited resources at their disposal. With programs like the Museum of Texas Tech University's Art with Emotion or the Wyoming Dinosaur Center's Shovel Ready, museums are meeting the challenges of this diverse audience and finding success in the variety of their programs.

Women in Science

Kenosha Public Museum, Kenosha, Wisconsin
Science/Art Museum
Open House
  Target Audience: Local community, multigenerational audience
  Attendance: More than 200 people
  Overview: For the Women in Science program, local resident scientists from multiple disciplines are invited to the museum to share their work with the public. Each scientist is provided space in a fair-style event and paired with simple, museum-planned, hands-on activities to generate additional interest and understanding. Visitors are able to meet each scientist, explore their work, and directly ask questions. Subsequent conversations allow scientists to garner public support for their work, while audience members experience the research happening in their community.
  Budget: $0
  Interpretive Components: ★★★★ Visitors have the opportunity to directly speak with each scientist about work being conducted. Many of the disciplines represented are not well known or are often misunderstood, and attending scientists can communicate with the public to encourage higher scientific understanding and support.

Staff Time Requirements: 20 hours. Staff time includes networking and recruiting scientists, marketing, and managing event logistics.

Audience Time Requirements: Flexible. Because of the open-house style of the program, audience members are free to explore the scientific areas that best capture their attention.

Scalability: ★★★★ The Women in Science program can accommodate as many scientists as there is interest and as many visitors as can safely fit in the host space.

Analysis: The Women in Science open house presents the museum as a liaison between the scientific community and museum visitors. It allows scientists to share their research with community members in digestible pieces, as visitors are flexible to explore presented fields depending on their interests. The museum further encourages scientific understanding by facilitating hands-on activities throughout the space. These activities help ensure content is available in multiple styles for any ability level.

While this particular event seems to tie best with organizations with a scientific mission, it could feasibly be adapted for any museum type. Historians, artists, craftspeople, and other researchers could be invited for similar open-house presentations. Museums willing to dedicate the time to network and recruit such representatives can feasibly adapt a comparable program to fit their needs.

Spycast

International Spy Museum, Washington, DC
History Museum
Podcast
  Target Audience: Online subscribers
  Attendance: More than 200 people

Credit: ©International Spy Museum

Figure 5.1 Recording the Spycast at the International Spy Museum

Overview: The International Spy Museum produces a regular online radio show, or podcast, available to online subscribers. Spycast uses interviews and programs with ex-spies, intelligence experts, and espionage scholars to explore the world of covert operations. These discussions provide detailed glimpses into a largely unknown field while often tying interview themes to museum collections and programs. The audio-only recordings are hosted by museum curator Dr. Vince Houghton and are available free to anyone online.

Budget: $0

Interpretive Components: ★★★★ Spycast recordings cover a variety of topics and perspectives related to spies and covert intelligence. They often directly relate to museum programs and exhibits and provide museum exposure well outside the normal marketing audience.

Staff Time Requirements: ~8 hours/recording. Staff time includes recruiting participants, scheduling, recording, and managing podcast details.

Audience Time Requirements: ~1 hour. Most recordings run about an hour in length.

Scalability: ★★★★★ Once the recording is produced, it is available for countless downloads online.

Analysis: Podcasts provide a unique opportunity to expand museum interpretation beyond traditional programs and exhibits. They further offer the museum an extensive but low-maintenance online presence, in that once the recording is complete, it requires little in the way of maintenance or upkeep. The International Spy Museum's Spycast extends the museum's reach to an international audience and drives interest in its collection and mission goals. For other museums interested in replicating this success, it must be noted that producing a podcast does have some technical requirements to manage the audio equipment and software. While there are several affordable and even free recording options, staff must know how to operate and manipulate each piece.

Japanese Name Interpretation Workshop

Japanese Cultural Center of Hawai'i, Honolulu, Hawaii
Cultural Center
Workshop

Target Audience: Those interested in Japanese culture and naming traditions

Attendance: 10–25 people

Overview: Four times a year, two volunteers from the Japanese Cultural Center of Hawai'i host a Japanese Name Interpretation Workshop. Focusing on first and middle names, the workshop explores the cultural

Credit: Japanese Cultural
Center of Hawai'i

*Figure 5.2 Japanese Name Interpretation Workshop participants at
the Japanese Cultural Center of Hawai'i*

and geographical significance, historical context, and naming trends associated with Japanese naming practices. Participants are even invited to
submit two names in advance to include in this discussion. At the workshop's conclusion, participants receive two cards with their submitted
names written in kanji. For many participants, this workshop provides
a direct tie to their family history and deepens personal connections and
experiences. This often translates to increased support for and involvement with the cultural center.

Budget: $0

Interpretive Components: ★★★★★ The workshop covers several
components of Japanese naming culture, including geography, history,
and common trends. Previously submitted names are even researched
and included in this discussion.

Staff Time Requirements: ~5 hours/workshop. While two volunteers
research and lead the workshop, museum staff handle marketing, participant registration, workshop correspondence, and event logistics.

Audience Time Requirements: 2 hours. The workshop runs a full two hours to include all components and have time for question and answers.

Scalability: ★★ Because of the personalized nature of this workshop, it would be incredibly difficult to host a larger participant audience. Larger groups would not be guaranteed the same level of engagement, nor would there be the time to research and prepare the personal name information.

Analysis: Much of the success of the Japanese Name Interpretation Workshop is because of the encouraged inclusion of personal family names. Workshop instructors research each name, providing a genealogical service for their participants. This added benefit takes the traditional instruction-based program and expands its reach to create personalized connections and develop deeper ancestral understandings. This approach can be replicated across multiple genealogic themes (e.g., other naming traditions, meanings, and geographies) as well as other museum-oriented themes. Workshops exploring other ethnic naming trends and distant ancestral connections or tracing object provenance and ownership could be just as successful.

Poetry N' Rhythm

Blanden Art Museum, Fort Dodge, Iowa
Art Museum
Event
   Target Audience: Spoken-word and other performing artists
   Attendance: 25–50 people

Credit: Blanden Art Museum

Figure 5.3 Poetry N' Rhythm at the Blanden Art Museum

Overview: Poetry N' Rhythm is a free monthly event where poets, musicians, storytellers, rappers, and other performing artists are encouraged to express themselves through spoken word and music. Each gathering is themed to direct content as performers share unique compositions and cover pieces. Artists are free to provide their own interpretation to their performed piece as they share their talent with the audience.

Budget: $0

Interpretive Components: ★★ While museum interpretation is very minimal, performers can share personal interpretations and understandings of their chosen pieces, often providing alternative perspectives for audience members.

Staff Time Requirements: 3 hours/event. This time includes planning and marketing the event to the artists.

Audience Time Requirements: 1 hour. Multiple artists perform throughout the one-hour event.

Scalability: ★★★★ Perhaps the biggest challenge in scaling this event comes with how big an audience the space can support. The ability to allow more (or fewer) artists to perform is simply addressed by adjusting the length of the event.

Analysis: Using the museum space to encourage performance art is not a new concept, but providing a recurring, open-mic-style event can seem intimidating and time consuming. However, these opportunities allow artists and audience members to experience the museum in new ways, helping them to associate the space as a safe place for self-expression and personal interpretation. For museums looking to replicate the event, it is an easy one to host, provided the museum has a place to house the audience and can establish the necessary network to attract the artists.

Twilight Tours

Conrad-Caldwell House Museum, Louisville, Kentucky
Historic House
Tour

Target Audience: Multigenerational audience

Attendance: 10–25 people

Overview: Each month over the summer, the Conrad-Caldwell House Museum offers two tours through the historic home during the evening and twilight hours. Led by docent volunteers, the tours offer unique opportunities to see the site in lower lighting. The tours also offer audience members who work during the day a chance to still explore the site through a guided experience.

Budget: $0

Credit: Conrad-Caldwell House Museum

Figure 5.4 Twilight Tours at the Conrad-Caldwell House Museum

Interpretive Components: ★★★ Twilight Tours are regular site tours offered during the evening hours. Docents share information about the site and its history throughout the scheduled tour.

Staff Time Requirements: ~2 hours. In addition to the volunteer docents, staff are available to oversee the tours and to help with necessary crowd control.

Audience Time Requirements: 75 minutes. Tours run just over an hour.

Scalability: ★★★ Twilight Tours can be run with a single audience member, but larger audiences must be split into multiple groups to fit in the museum spaces. This requires additional docents and staggered tour times to keep groups separated for noise and movement.

Analysis: In many ways, the Twilight Tours are a simple matter of keeping a site open later than normally advertised. Tour scripts are unchanged, and exhibit spaces are untouched. The only difference is that the tours are offered later in the evening. This allows audience members otherwise unable to visit the site a chance to explore and experience the museum. This concept of later, evening tours is a simple addition any museum can adapt. As long as staff are available, tours and other museum programs can be offered after normal business hours.

Nicole Carson Bonilla: A Cowgirl's Legacy

Western Spirit: Scottsdale's Museum of the West, Scottsdale, Arizona
History Museum
Lecture
   Target Audience: Multigenerational audience
   Attendance: 50–100 people
   Overview: Hosted by the Western Spirit museum, Nicole Carson Bonilla shares her personal story of growing up among a family of Western show performers. With information dating to the 1930s and covering stories about her grandfather Buss Carson, her father's Carson Family Western Show, and her own children, she shares photographs, video, and objects pertaining to her life. This presentation explores the changing dynamic of Western performers through the lens of one woman's experience and allows audience members the opportunity to see this world through her life.
   Budget: $0
   Interpretive Components: ★★★★ The breadth of information covers several decades of western performances, including venues, performance types (e.g., trick roping, dog acts, etc.), and objects relating to Ms. Bonilla's life, many never before available for public viewing.
   Staff Time Requirements: ~20 hours. The majority of this time is spent developing a relationship with Ms. Bonilla and encouraging her to share her story. There is also some minimal setup and cleanup associated with the event.
   Audience Time Requirements: 1 hour. This program runs one hour, including a question-and-answer period at the end of the scheduled program.
   Scalability: ★★★★ Because the lecture is held in the museum theater, it could easily accommodate a larger audience. Smaller audiences could be moved to a smaller space with little effect on the program.
   Analysis: Every community contains characters with unexpected and even surprising stories. These life histories provide commentary and new viewpoints on historic narratives and changing community cultures. Museums like the Western Spirit can greatly benefit from these people, as they are often willing to not only share their personal stories but also do it without financial compensation. While it may take time to identify and develop relationships with these individuals, museums willing to foster such networks can grow their programming, exhibit, and even operational options.

Sergeant York Film Viewing

Museum Center at 5ive Points, Cleveland, Tennessee
History Museum
Event
   Target Audience: Multigenerational audience
   Attendance: $0
   Overview: Using the temporary exhibit *War Memorials* as inspiration, the Museum Center at 5ive Points hosted a viewing of Gary Cooper's 1941 public-domain film *Sergeant York*. Both before and after the two-plus hour film, audience members were encouraged to share their memories and personal stories of wartime.
   Budget: $0
   Interpretive Components: ★★★ Following the film's biopic approach, staff led spectators in informal conversations and stories to enhance the film's interpretation and relevance to both the exhibit and audience members' lives.
   Staff Time Requirements: 4 hours. Time includes planning, setting up, and cleanup, in addition to the film.
   Audience Time Requirements: ~2.5 hours. *Sergeant York* runs just over two hours, in addition to audience conversations.
   Scalability: ★★★★★ The biggest limitation on audience size is space and the audiovisual equipment. As long as the space can accommodate large audiences and these spectators can all see and hear the film, potential audience size is virtually unlimited.
   Analysis: Films are a common, low-maintenance programming option that generally attract a good crowd. The Museum Center at 5ive Points improves this program model by tying the film to a current exhibit and encouraging audience members to contribute their own experiences before and after the film. This helps connect the movie to both the museum and the attendees. While this film showing was based on an historic exhibit, any museum can find films, documentaries, and features to fit its mission and collection. For museums looking to add film viewings to their programming plans, it must be noted that the *Sergeant York* viewing was kept under budget because it is in the public domain. For any film not in the public domain, a viewing license must be obtained through an official film distributor or licensor. Depending on the film selected, this can run several hundred dollars per showing.

How to Make Sauerkraut

German American Heritage Center, Davenport, Iowa
Cultural Center
Workshop
   Target Audience: Multigenerational audience
   Attendance: 10–25 people
   Overview: Hosted by the German American Heritage Center, the How to Make Sauerkraut workshop provides a step-by-step tutorial on how to prepare the dish. It includes hands-on processes, recipes, and information on the German culture's use of the food. The workshop allows participants to explore food philosophies as well as provides the recipes for home use.
   Budget: $0
   Interpretive Components: ★★★★ The workshop includes discussions on the culinary history and cultural components of sauerkraut as well as how to make it.
   Staff Time Requirements: ~2 hours. Staff time includes marketing, setup, and cleanup.
   Audience Time Requirements: ~1 hour. The workshop runs about an hour for all culinary steps to be completed.
   Scalability: ★★★ Hands-on workshops do best with smaller audiences; however, larger groups can be accommodated with multiple station areas, more materials, and occasionally additional instructors.
   Analysis: Food-based programming provides unique opportunities to explore history, culture, art, and even scientific processes through a familiar theme. They can be successful in not only drawing large audiences but also connecting participants to museum interpretation and collection objects. However, these food-based programs have a few more special requirements than other programming types. Sinks, ovens, and easy-to-clean floors, among other things, can make them more of a programmatic challenge. Still, goods like sauerkraut have minimal kitchen requirements, making them easier to adapt to museum education spaces.

Flax: From Plant to Thread

Amherst Historical Society, Amherst, Massachusetts
History Museum
Demonstration
   Target Audience: Multigenerational audience
   Attendance: 10–25 people
   Overview: To highlight several antique flax-processing tools in the Simeon Strong House collection, the Amherst Historical Society hosts a

volunteer craftsman to demonstrate the process of preparing flax for spinning into yarn or thread. Visitors can not only watch the process, but they also can work with the materials themselves. During the demonstration, they are able to use multiple tools with corresponding displayed pieces, as well as learn how the material ties into several museum exhibit themes. The demonstration is available for several hours and allows visitors to come and go as they please.

Budget: $10

Interpretive Components: ★★★★ The demonstration allows visitors to witness the historic process, discuss the historic and contemporary components of the craft, and attempt to prepare the flax using hand tools. This demonstration appeals to multiple learning styles and gives visitors the opportunity to explore at their own pace.

Staff Time Requirements: ~8 hours. This includes recruiting, planning, marketing, and event logistics, like setup and cleanup. The demonstration runs for three hours.

Audience Time Requirements: Flexible. Because the Flax: From Plant to Thread demonstration runs for the full scheduled time, visitors are given the freedom to spend as much or as little time as they please. Some stay for only a few minutes, while others stay for more than an hour.

Scalability: ★★★ This program can easily accommodate different size audiences as long as the space is large enough. However, a larger audience may require multiple craftsmen to distribute visitors and reduce crowding.

Analysis: Demonstrations are a great way to tie museum collections and historic processes to audience experience. Visitors are free to explore the shown activity in whatever capacity they wish, either through observation, discussion, or even occasional hands-on interaction. These activities can be led by museum staff or volunteer craftsmen, and they can be as interactive as space, materials, and methods allow. Any museum, regardless of collection type, can adapt appropriate demonstrations to illustrate displayed objects and interpretive concepts.

Meet the Artist

Alutiiq Museum and Archaeology Repository, Kodiak, Alaska
History/Art/Culture Museum
Community Exhibit/Partnership/Demonstration

Target Audience: Kodiak community and cruise line tourists

Attendance: 25–50 people

Overview: The Alutiiq Museum and Archaeology Repository regularly invites local artists to display their work in the museum gallery. During this time, artists meet visitors, sell their work, and demonstrate the pro-

Figure 5.5 June Pardue shares her artwork and jewelry at the Alutiiq Museum, Kodiak, Alaska, through the Meet the Artist program

cesses involved with their art. Often, the event corresponds with the local First Friday art walk. On some occasions, the event occurs when a cruise ship is in port, allowing potentially hundreds of people to connect with the artists and the traditional art forms they practice. Refreshments are occasionally included.

Budget: $15

Interpretive Components: ★★★ Patrons are invited to interact directly with the artists, asking questions, examining the artwork, and exploring the process through demonstrations. This encourages personal engagement and deeper learning.

Staff Time Requirements: 4 hours. Staff time includes the two-hour event, cleaning up, and marketing.

Audience Time Requirements: Flexible. Museum visitors have the flexibility to spend as much or as little time with the artists as they please.

Scalability: ★★★★ This event can support as many visitors as the space allows. In fact, for cruise ship days, the Alutiiq Museum will often invite multiple artists and set them up in the larger atrium to handle a crowd of 200 to 300 people throughout the day.

Analysis: Inviting local artists and craftspeople to display and demonstrate their arts has the dual purpose of connecting museum collections with active artistic processes and providing the chance to promote and even sell the artist's work. Visitors are able to directly communicate with the artists, learning both the history and components of related processes. They can then mark this experience by purchasing displayed work. This not only supports the local economy through direct sales, but it also fosters the museum's image in the artistic community while driving audience visitation. This mutually beneficial partnership provides a successful programming model while stimulating artistic awareness. Museums interested in exploring this partnership should be ready to develop and nurture the necessary relationships with the local artistic community.

1 in 10

Shelburne Museum, Shelburne, Vermont
History / Art Museum
In-Gallery
   Target Audience: Museum visitors
   Attendance: More than 200 people
   Overview: The 1 in 10 program allows Shelburne gallery guides to explore a selected artist, artwork, or theme during a 10-minute discussion with museum visitors. These presentations are set throughout the day and encourage visitors to explore museum exhibits through a short, semiguided conversation and program. Gallery guides research and refine their chosen topics throughout the season and receive additional training as needed.
   Budget: ~$20
   Interpretive Components: ★★★★ Because gallery guides choose their own focuses, they are able to develop their programs based on personal strengths and interests. This encourages deeper audience engagement and discussion.
   Staff Time Requirements: ~60 hours. Staff time includes initial meetings with guides and ongoing coaching to refine each program. Volunteer guides conduct two programs per day over the summer.
   Audience Time Requirements: ~10 minutes. Each 1 in 10 program is designed to last 10 minutes, but the time can be altered depending on audience interest.
   Scalability: ★★ This program is designed for intimate discussions with small groups of visitors. While the space can accommodate larger groups, the likelihood for the same engaged, comfortable conversation greatly diminishes.

Analysis: The 1 in 10 program allows museum docents to follow and develop their own interests and then to share these interests with visitors using small, personal conversations. Encouraging volunteers to identify and deepen their own passions for the museum's collection ensures their investment and support of both the museum and their individual programs. Permitting visitors to glimpse this dedication and passion sparks their own curiosity and interest in the selected pieces and can lead to more meaningful interpretive opportunities and experiences. Other museums could easily replicate this programmatic success by simply allowing their volunteers to identify and share which objects and stories capture their interest, and asking staff to host similar 10 minute conversations focusing on a single piece or theme is an easy, low-maintenance program model.

Baldwin Home Candlelight Tour

Lahaina Restoration Foundation, Maui, Hawaii
Historic Site
Tour
    Target Audience: After-hours visitors, multigenerational audience
    Attendance: 10–25 people

Figure 5.6 Jackie Hala and the Candlelight Tour at the Baldwin Home

Overview: This tour allows visitors to explore the historic Baldwin Home at dusk, after the home usually closes to the public. Led by docents, the candlelight (or flashlight) tour uses stories and objects to share the site's history. In addition to making the museum available to those not able to visit during regular hours, the flashlight tour provides a slightly different focus by narrowing attention on certain details and room features. This encourages visitors to see the historic site in a different light, both literally and figuratively.

Budget: $20

Interpretive Components: ★★★ Much of the tour is adapted from the regular tour provided during open hours but with the novelty of slightly darkened spaces and flashlights. Tour guides are even inspired to include supplemental information throughout the program.

Staff Time Requirements: 4 hours. This includes planning and prep for the tours, managing the visitors, and cleaning up.

Audience Time Requirements: 30 minutes. The Candlelight Tour runs about a half-hour.

Scalability: ★★★ Space in the historic home can only manage smaller groups; however larger groups can be split into multiple tours.

Analysis: The Baldwin House Candlelight Tour takes the opportunity to explore usual interpretive space under different lighting. While this seems like a small change, it provides a subtle shift in perspective as it focuses attention to particular tour topics and spotlights specific exhibit details. This, in addition to docent's ability to enhance tour information with extra stories and facts, provides a clever programming alternative without a high staff or resource commitment. These simple changes can be easily adapted to any facility looking for similar low-maintenance tour alternatives.

Echoes of the Past Cemetery Tours

Johnson County Jim Gatchell Memorial Museum, Buffalo, Wyoming
History Museum
Tour / Off-Site

Target Audience: Local multigenerational community

Attendance: More than 200 people

Overview: The nighttime, lantern-led Echoes of the Past Cemetery Tours take the audience through the local cemetery, where they meet volunteer interpreters portraying historic characters. These characters are either buried in the cemetery, have long histories with the community, or are archetypes of the area (e.g., anonymous cowboy, woman of the plains, etc.). Audience members can interact with each character through questions and conversations as the actors maintain their roles throughout the dialogue. This not only provides a fun experience, but it also helps to deepen interpretation and historic understandings.

Budget: $25

Credit: Johnson County Jim Gatchell Memorial Museum

Figure 5.7 Echoes of the Past Cemetery volunteers

Interpretive Components: ★★★★ Each volunteer is responsible for researching and composing the script for their characters using archival materials and historic photographs. There is often a direct correlation between the quality of information and the volunteers' investment in their characters. For example, volunteers portraying ancestors can include family lore and private documents to deepen the interpretation.

Staff Time Requirements: 176 hours. This program requires a massive time investment from staff and volunteers. In addition to researching and writing the scripts, planning and marketing the event, and creating costumes, volunteers must attend several hours of rehearsals to finalize their portrayals. Most tours have five to six "spirits," but additional characters can be rotated through each night.

Audience Time Requirements: 2.5 hours. Walking tours run two and a half hours, but sometimes shorter tours are made available.

Scalability: ★★★★ The Echoes of the Past Cemetery Tours can accommodate any size audience. While small group tours are ideal for the audience to engage with the "spirits," larger groups can be broken into smaller tours and spread across the cemetery, depending on how many characters are portrayed.

Analysis: The Echoes of the Past Cemetery Tours provide the Jim Gatchell Memorial Museum and its volunteers the chance to apply the history and stories of the community in a fun, entertaining program. With their program responsibilities, volunteers develop their own connections to their selected characters and explore ways to display the unique personalities and traits they discover with their audience. The ultimate success of the program is heavily dependent on this dedicated volunteer base and their willingness to learn and portray their characters. Without it, the program cannot happen. Because of their efforts, audience members are presented with an entertaining program that blends historic interpretation with theatrical performance and a unique atmosphere.

Star Parties

Grout Museum District, Waterloo, Iowa
History/Art/Science Museum
Open House/Partnership
   Target Audience: Multigenerational audience
   Attendance: 10–25 people
   Overview: Every month, the Grout Museum District hosts a Star Party, where visitors explore the night sky using binoculars and telescopes provided by the local astronomy club. Visitors are also invited to bring their own instruments to share. The events tie closely to planetarium programming and interpretation and allow visitors to learn about the astronomical sciences while interacting with the lenses and instruments used to view the skies. Regularly hosting the event adds deeper interpretive opportunities, as changes in star and constellation positions can be observed. Additional activities for children provide an added layer of learning for multigenerational groups.
   Budget: $30
   Interpretive Components: ★★★ With ties to the planetarium and the local astronomy club, interpretation on constellations and planets and the science of observing them are covered during each Star Party.
   Staff Time Requirements: 2 hours/event. Each event requires setup, manning the event, cleanup, and marketing.
   Audience Time Requirements: Flexible. During each Star Party, telescopes are arranged around the grounds, and audience members are free to come and go as they please.
   Scalability: ★★★ The event is very easy to scale to fit any museum outdoor space. The biggest hurdle to a larger audience is whether enough telescopes can be acquired for audience use.
   Analysis: These monthly Star Parties invite visitors to view, learn about, and discuss the night sky regardless of their previous experience levels.

By encouraging any knowledgeable astronomers and novice community members to attend, the Grout Museum District offers a free, open forum for participants to mingle and explore together. In this way, the museum relinquishes much of its control of the program and allows interpretation and learning to happen freely. Their willingness to do so creates a relaxed and flexible atmosphere that encourages self-guided discovery. Museums looking to replicate this program should be willing to experiment with giving up similar control. This is, of course, in addition to finding access to the needed viewing instruments.

Museum Collection Protection: Gallery Cleaning

Indiana State Museum and Historic Sites, Indianapolis, Indiana
History Museum
Demonstration
   Target Audience: Visitors to the Indiana State Museum and Historic Sites
   Attendance: More than 200 people

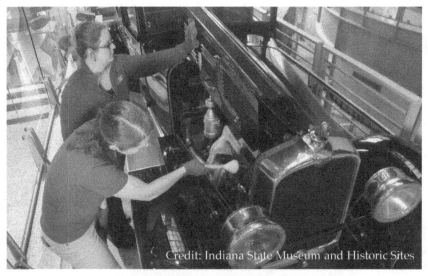

Figure 5.8 Museum Collection Protection:
Gallery Cleaning at the Indiana State Museum

   Overview: Every month, museum staff provide a behind-the-scenes glimpse of museum operations through a gallery cleaning demonstration. Through this demonstration, staff explain the museum's responsibilities to its collection and the stewardship involved. Staff show proper object-handling techniques, introduce which cleaning tools are needed, and exhibit how these tools are used. Further discussion on proper environment is also addressed, explaining why food and drink are not allowed in museum galleries.

Budget: ~$50

Interpretive Components: ★★★★ The Museum Collection Protection program offers the opportunity to interpret museums rather than the collection objects. Staff model basic object-handling best practices, and museum preservation themes are expressed during each session.

Staff Time Requirements: 7 hours/month. The one-hour sessions are scheduled daily for one week every month.

Audience Time Requirements: Flexible. Because the demonstrations rotate through gallery spaces and combine audience discussions with actual gallery cleaning, visitors are free to come and go as they please.

Scalability: ★★★ This program works best with smaller audiences to ensure easy staff–visitor conversations. Larger audience needs would be harder to meet for visibility and conversations, but the program could feasibly be transferred to nongallery spaces and expanded to include lectures to accommodate these needs.

Analysis: It is obvious that museum exhibits must be cleaned regularly. Conducting these cleanings during open hours and inviting audience viewing and questions are a simple adjustment. The Indiana State Museum and Historic Sites has adopted this program model to educate visitors on the museum, its collection, and all that is involved in maintaining and preserving the objects. The demonstration provides a glimpse into museum operations through an easily executed program. Any museum could duplicate these efforts by simply cleaning during open hours and providing time to discuss staff actions with interested visitors.

Shovel Ready

Wyoming Dinosaur Center, Thermopolis, Wyoming
Science Museum
Off-Site

Target Audience: Multigenerational audience interested in paleontology

Attendance: 100–200 people

Overview: Shovel Ready allows visitors to be paleontologists for an afternoon. Participants are transported to an active dinosaur quarry, where they receive basic training and information before they are allowed to excavate under the supervision of their own paleontological guides. The program includes a tour of the site and hands-on excavation as participants assist site staff in completing regular field assignments.

Figure 5.9 Shovel Ready with the Wyoming Dinosaur Center

Budget: $50

Interpretive Components: ★★★★ Each program involves a tour of an active dinosaur excavation, discussion of the scientific aspects of paleontology, and hands-on excavation of prehistoric fossils. Participants are encouraged to ask questions throughout the program.

Staff Time Requirements: ~4 hours. Site staff must train and supervise program participants in addition to preparing for their arrival. Cleanup is incorporated into the program schedule.

Audience Time Requirements: 3 hours. Each program runs for three hours at the excavation site.

Scalability: ★★★ Because preregistration is required, staff are given notice when larger groups are coming. Additional participants require more excavation tools and may require extra staff.

Analysis: Shovel Ready provides the opportunity for interested participants—regardless of age or ability—to experience an active paleontological excavation. Through hands-on training and site involvement, participants are able to experience the paleontological field with active immersion in excavation work. This not only provides a unique experience, but it also offers volunteer workers to help with site efforts. While this particular program is dependent on an accessible site, the program components of immersing participants in fieldwork can be adapted to any discipline. Archaeology, biology, environmental science, or even public art could all be feasibly tapped for similar program models.

Art with Emotion

Museum of Texas Tech University, Lubbock, Texas
History / Science / Art / Culture Museum
In-Gallery / Workshop

   Target Audience: Audiences on the autism spectrum
   Attendance: Less than 10 people
   Overview: Art with Emotion uses art and color to build body language and emotion recognition for individuals on the autism spectrum. Many people with autism struggle with recognizing emotion and body cues in others. This program allows them to explore how different emotions connect to body language, helping them to better connect socially with others. Each program explores a different emotion through individual gallery works and concludes with a workshop activity where participants can express that emotion artistically.

Credit: Bethany Cheshire

Figure 5.10 "Anger Monsters" by Art with Emotion participants

Budget: $50

Interpretive Components: ★★★ The gallery component of Art with Emotion depends on shared interpretation, where program staff and participants are equal partners in discussing the art and emotions it conveys. Participants are able to explore and express their own reactions to each piece with support rather than instruction from staff.

Staff Time Requirements: 8 hours. Time includes planning, activity preparation, manning the program, and cleaning up.

Audience Time Requirements: ~1.5 hours/program. Each program runs about an hour and a half for both the gallery and activity components. Because each program explores a different emotion, participants are free to attend any one or all sessions.

Scalability: ★ The success of Art with Emotion program depends on participants being comfortable sharing their thoughts and observations. This is predicated on small, familiar groups.

Analysis: Unfortunately, museums often ignore the programming needs of audience members on the autism spectrum, and many programs that do target this group simply offer current exhibits or activities in a low-sensory environment without adapting program content to specifically meet this audience's unique learning and development needs. Art with Emotion is explicitly designed to meet these needs and to foster skills that translate to real-world interactions. The workshop's success is greatly dependent on this singular focus.

While the workshop's success is inspiring, there are several challenges with duplicating the Art with Emotion program. Museums must have an accessible art collection that elicits a range of emotions. While other collection types could be used to explore the development of other skills, emotions and body language are best explored through art. Museum staff must also be willing to lead the special needs participants through the program components. This may require extra training.

Stars and Stardust: Sidewalk Astronomy in the Neon Boneyard

Neon Museum, Las Vegas, Nevada
Art/History Museum
Open House/Partnership

Target Audience: Urban stargazers, multigenerational audience

Overview: The Neon Museum partners with the Las Vegas Astronomical Society and the College of Southern Nevada Planetarium to provide telescopes and activities for viewing the night sky. Set in the Neon Boneyard, where the museum's outdoor sign collection is displayed, participants are able to use several professional telescopes, complete a self-paced solar system scavenger hunt, and create a planisphere.

Figure 5.11 Stars and Stardust: Sidewalk Astronomy in the Neon Boneyard at the Neon Museum

Budget: $50

Interpretive Components: ★★★ Interpretation is offered throughout the program depending on audience interest. Themes cover astronomy and artistic and scientific properties of light, scale, distance, and proportion.

Staff Time Requirements: 20 hours. This time includes cultivating relationships and communicating with the partnering institutions, as well as planning, setup, and cleanup.

Audience Time Requirements: Flexible. While audience members are welcome to come and go as they please, the event runs for three hours.

Scalability: ★★★★★ The open nature of this program can accommodate an untold number of participants, as long as space is available. Having multiple activities available also allows the audience to rotate through and eliminates crowding around the telescopes.

Analysis: Through the help of its partners, the Neon Museum is able to focus the Stars and Stardust event on interpretation and museum-planned activities. Rather than invite community astronomers to share their own knowledge, the museum takes the lead in facilitating discussions, offering educational activities, and sparking astronomical discoveries. This creates a fun, informative environment for groups to explore the night sky. Museums interested in duplicating this program can explore the extent of their interpretive involvement during the planning stages.

Fossil Dig

Aurora Fossil Museum Foundation, Aurora, North Carolina
Science Museum
Off-Site/Activity-Based
   Target Audience: Local community groups
   Attendance: 25–50 people

Figure 5.12 Fossil Dig with the Aurora Fossil Museum Foundation, Inc.

Overview: Offered both remotely and on-site, the Fossil Dig program uses exhibits, specialized lectures, and fossil-digging activities to explore the geologic history and local fossil record. Fossils donated by a local phosphorus mining company are used in trays for participants to actively search for the pieces under discussion. The mobile option provides off-site groups the same opportunity to excavate.
   Budget: $75
   Interpretive Components: ★★★ The Fossil Dig program allows participants to experience a paleontological excavation without traveling to a dig site. Fossil exploration and specially geared lectures ensure the information is appropriate and engaging for audience members.

Staff Time Requirements: 3 hours. Staff time includes delivery, setup, instruction and engagement, and cleanup.

Audience Time Requirements: ~45 minutes. The program can run anywhere from 30 minutes to an hour, depending on participants' needs.

Scalability: ★★★ Fossil Dig can be adapted for any size audience. Simply add more trays and fossils for the activity component.

Analysis: The Fossil Dig program simulates a paleontological dig to provide participants the experience of digging for fossils without the trip to an active excavation site. The program's digging components imitate excavation processes and offer hands-on, interactive involvement with the geological and paleontological discussions. Museums looking to replicate this program can do so with minimal material costs, as long as fossils can be obtained inexpensively.

Learning about Your Past

Rutherford B. Hayes Presidential Library & Museum, Fremont, Ohio
History Museum/Library
Workshop
  Target Audience: Family historians, multigenerational audience
  Attendance: 25–50 per class

Credit: Rutherford B. Hayes Presidential Library & Museum

Figure 5.13 Learning about Your Past with the Rutherford B. Hayes Presidential Library & Museum

Overview: Learning about *Your* Past is a monthly genealogy class to assist family historians in their research. Each class covers a different component of family history, including beginning genealogy, digital and historic photography, compiling family history books, and free and paid genealogical resources both online and at the museum. Audience members are free to attend whichever sessions they desire.

Budget: $75

Interpretive Components: ★★★ Each class covers a different aspect of family genealogy, providing a comprehensive overview to family research efforts.

Staff Time Requirements: ~6 hours/program. Staff time includes setting up, facilitating, and cleaning up for each program. It also includes additional preparation time for first-time class topics.

Audience Time Requirements: 2 hours. Each class runs approximately two hours.

Scalability: ★★★★ The biggest limitation on class size is space logistics. Class content can be taught to a few participants, or it can be tailored for a much larger class.

Analysis: Genealogical research is a growing field for museums, and the introduction of new resources and digital tools can make it a complicated one. The Learning about *Your* Past workshop uses staff knowledge to equip family historians so they discover their own ancestry. This not only prepares participants for their own research, but it also advertises museum services and improves the quality of future museum requests. Museums willing to put in the time to plan and develop similar workshop sessions could easily see the same benefits.

Panel Discussion on Race and Ethnicity

Moody Museum, Taylor, Texas
Historic Site
Event/Partnership

Target Audience: Adults and teens

Attendance: 50–100 people

Overview: After the success of several individual panel discussions with panelists representing major community groups, including African American, Hispanic, and Anglo community members, the Moody Museum hosted a combined, public panel discussion divided by gender and ethnicity. The museum partnered with sophomore teachers at a community high school, who assigned essays on the same topics. The top five essays were then read by the students during the program.

Budget: $95

Credit: Moody Museum

Figure 5.14 Panel Discussion on Race and Ethnicity at the Moody Museum

Interpretive Components: ★★★★ Using several panelists and stu dents ensures that multiple perspectives are explored throughout the program. This encourages a deeper exploration into community and national gender and ethnic discussions.

Staff Time Requirements: ~18 hours. Each individual panel is held to one hour, and the public presentation lasts two hours. This, in addition to setup, cleanup, panelist recruitment, and essay judging, make up the staff time requirement.

Audience Time Requirements: ~2 hours. The public program component lasts approximately two hours and includes the panel discussion, reading essays, questions and answers, and time for refreshments

Scalability: ★★★ This event can be scaled smaller or larger, depending on how many community panelists and student essayists are involved.

Analysis: The Moody Museum not only tackles challenging and sometimes controversial topics through these panel discussions, but they also accomplished this while involving high-schoolers. This intentional approach expands the program's social reach while making the museum relevant to each community group involved. Discussions are multifaceted, as different perspectives stemming from age, gender, ethnicity, and community are shared. This helps deepen understanding and ensures personal connections for participants. While the social success of the program is exciting, replicating it could be a significant challenge. In addition to nurturing community buy-in and inviting youth involvement, museums must be willing to create safe spaces to enable these challenging conversations.

Thursday Night Lineup

Brucemore, Inc., Cedar Rapids, Iowa
Historic Site
Tour
   Target Audience: After-hours, multigenerational audience
   Attendance: 100–200 people

Figure 5.15 Thursday Night Lineup tours at Brucemore, Inc.

Overview: During the spring and fall, Brucemore, Inc., offers three after-hours tours in their Thursday Night Lineup program. Each tour highlights a special perspective of the site not included in the normal guided tour. These include an in-depth exploration of the architecture and the closed spaces of the mansion, a landscape and garden walk, and a tour offered from the perspective of mansion servants. Each offers an alternative interpretive perspective, as well as making the site available to visitors who are unable to come during regular open hours.
   Budget: ~$100
   Interpretive Components: ★★★★ Each tour offered in the Thursday Night Lineup builds on the information given during a regular guided

tour. They continue to explore the site's history and grounds through differing perspectives and unique access to spaces normally unavailable to the public.

Staff Time Requirements: ~3 hours/week. Time includes registering tour visitors, printing materials, and preparing the house for the tour.

Audience Time Requirements: 1.5 hours. Each tour runs an hour and a half to cover the themed spaces.

Scalability: ★★★ Because of the historic spaces included on the tours, groups are limited to 15 people. However, larger groups could be accommodated with additional tour times.

Analysis: Rather than focus on behind-the-scenes spaces, the Thursday Night Lineup intentionally offers detailed interpretation in exhibit spaces not normally covered in a tour, often from alternative viewpoints. The program ensures that every character's story is included in site interpretation. This not only deepens educational opportunities, but by offering them after hours once a week, staff are also able to dedicate the planning and development time necessary to create singular programming experiences. Other museums, regardless of organization type, could adapt similar after-hours tours exploring alternate perspectives, behind-the-scenes spaces, and museum grounds.

Historical Craft Society

History Colorado Center, Denver, Colorado
History Museum
Workshop/Social Club

   Target Audience: Multigenerational audience

   Attendance: 10–25 people

   Overview: The Historical Craft Society uses historic items from the museum collection to inspire craft projects and activities. Each meeting includes the craft, conversation, and refreshments. Depending on the activity, museum staff and professional craftspeople are available to help instruct and guide the hands-on learning process. The program has included cupcake decorating, weaving, embroidery, paper beads, decoupage, and even pumpkin carving.

   Budget: $100

   Interpretive Components: ★★★ While historic objects from the collection are used for inspiration, the program is focused on the chosen craft activity. Instruction and interpretation center on the process and methods for that specific craft.

   Staff Time Requirements: ~7 hours/meeting. Time includes planning, preparation, and cleanup, in addition to manning the program. Additional time may be required, depending on that program's needs.

Audience Time Requirements: 2 hours. Each program meeting runs two hours.

Scalability: ★★ The hands-on aspects of the Historical Craft Society demand smaller group sizes. Larger audiences present greater challenges in meeting individual instruction and material needs.

Analysis: The Historical Craft Society uses the museum's collection and local instructors to inspire hands-on instruction in a social atmosphere. Club members gather for socialization and collaboration and to learn new crafts and processes. In this manner, the program satisfies multiple audience needs while exploring relevant, fun themes. While the regular meetings require a large staff time commitment to plan, develop, recruit, and man the program, the recurring gathering provides consistent visitor satisfaction and garners continued audience support for the museum and its programming efforts.

How to Make Hypertufa Pots

Chieftains Museum/Major Ridge Home, Rome, Georgia
Historic Site/History Museum
Workshop/Partnership
    Target Audience: Multigenerational audience
    Attendance: 1–25 people

Credit: Chieftains Museum/Major Ridge Home

Figure 5.16 Making hypertufa pots at the Chieftains Museum/Major Ridge Home

Overview: The Chieftains Museum partners with the Floyd County Master Gardeners organization to host the How to Make Hypertufa Pots workshop. Master gardeners volunteer to lead participants through the process of creating rustic, textured containers using concrete and local plant materials. Participants experiment with the process and creation of these pots through hands-on instruction, and many of the workshop materials and the concrete mixer are donated to help reduce costs.

Budget: $100

Interpretive Components: ★★ While local-area plants and their uses are discussed during the workshop, much of the focus is on the process and methods of creating the hypertufa pots.

Staff Time Requirements: ~9 hours. Although most of the planning and work for the program is done by volunteers, it does take eight master gardeners to run the program.

Audience Time Requirements: 1 hour. The workshop runs approximately an hour.

Scalability: ★★★ Because the program requires preregistration, the amount of material and staff needed are always known. However, larger groups require additional staffing, space, and materials to run the workshop.

Analysis: The How to Make Hypertufa Pots workshop is an example of using a community partnership to introduce participants to an involved and complex process. While some may find the pots too complicated in the way of materials and instruction to host such a program, the Chieftains Museum has been able to leverage their local community to provide the expertise and donated materials to make the workshop a reality. This allows the museum to provide the desired programming without overwhelming staff or financial resources. Other museums can find similar workshop success—although maybe not specifically for hypertufa pots—by identifying other dedicated volunteer bases willing to provide the necessary skills and program components.

Below the Scenes

Mai Wah Society and Museum, Butte, Montana
Culture/History Museum
Tour

Target Audience: Multigenerational audience

Attendance: 50–100 people

Overview: Housed in a 19th-century building, the Mai Wah Society's Below the Scenes tour highlights the lower basement rooms previously unavailable to museum visitors. The guided tour explores the construction and architecture of the site, how the building's use has changed over time, and how the building's inhabitants left their mark on the space, specifically touching on influence of Chinese residents. The tour ties the organization's mission to share the history, culture, and conditions of Asian people in the Rocky Mountains with the building that houses the Mai Wah Society.

Budget: $100

Interpretive Components: ★★★ Using the selected rooms, the tour explores the Asian Rocky Mountain experience through the lens of site architecture and habitation.

Staff Time Requirements: ~4 hours. Staff time includes designing the tour, preparing the space, and marketing the program.

Audience Time Requirements: 1 hour. The tour runs one hour.

Scalability: ★★★ The Below the Scenes tour can handle as many people as the space allows. Larger groups can be split among multiple tour times.

Analysis: It can be easy to forget that the museum building has its own story. Looking at the building as its own exhibit can explore architecture, building use history, and the people associated with the space. This not only extends the museum's collection to include structural features, but it also has the potential to deepen contextual and experiential museum mission components. Using a tour format like the Below the Scenes program, many different museums can connect their buildings to their missions and their collections.

Hands-On History Carts

Oklahoma History Center, Oklahoma City, Oklahoma
History Museum
In-Gallery

Target Audience: All visitors to the Oklahoma History Center

Attendance: More than 200 people

Overview: Using objects in the Education Collection, Oklahoma History Center volunteers man Hands-On History Carts throughout the museum galleries. Each cart includes objects that connect the exhibits to other story lines. Visitors can handle the artifacts and engage with volunteers about the gallery's exhibits, deepening interpretive understandings and encouraging connections to personal experiences.

Budget: $100

Interpretive Components: ★★★ Each cart builds on the information provided in each exhibit while allowing visitors to engage and interact with items similar to the ones on display. This helps them to connect overarching historic themes and events to relative and personal experience.

Credit: Oklahoma History Center

Figure 5.17 Hands-on History Carts at the Oklahoma History Center

Staff Time Requirements: ~6 hours/cart. Staff must research and compile the objects for each cart. Volunteers must be aware of all objects on their carts and know how to engage visitors, both with the objects and with the exhibits. Each manned cart is available in the galleries for three-hour shifts.

Audience Time Requirements: Flexible. Visitors are free to explore each cart at their own pace. Handling the objects and talking with the volunteers can encompass only a few minutes, or it can stretch for a significant amount of time.

Scalability: ★★★★★ The Hands-On History Carts can handle large numbers of people in a short amount of time. As long as the volunteers are familiar with how to manage the audience, visitors can freely cycle through the space.

Analysis: Tactile exploration has long been recognized in the museum field as an easy way to deepen exhibit connections, but the Oklahoma History Center builds on this program model by placing trained volunteers at each touch station. Their presence encourages questions and discussions about each piece and provides the opportunity to expand exhibit information as they facilitate interpretive connections and urge object interaction. While a manned object cart is relatively simple to institute, success depends on the ability of staff and docents to present a welcoming and encouraging façade and recognize interpretive opportunities.

Strolling with the Spirits

Grout Museum District, Waterloo, Iowa
Art/History/Science Museum
Tour
Target Audience: Multigenerational audience
Attendance: 50–100 people
Overview: Strolling with the Spirits is a walking tour through local cemeteries. Volunteer actors portraying famous or important historic figures share life stories and contextual historic information in front of corresponding headstones. These tours are often themed with different characters and occur throughout the year. For example, the 2017 Strolling with the Spirits tours included veteran stories and were focused around World War I and World War II anniversaries.
Budget: $100
Interpretive Components: ★★★★ Each actor brings their character to life through costume, mannerisms, and voice. Because each spirit walk includes multiple characters, participants are exposed to several different historic perspectives.
Staff Time Requirements: ~60 hours. Staff time includes recruiting actors, writing scripts, and leading tours. While some actors prefer to write their own scripts, removing the responsibility from staff members, the time required to plan, market, and lead the event is still time consuming.
Audience Time Requirements: ~75 minutes. Tours run between an hour to an hour and a half, depending on how many characters are included.
Scalability: ★★★★ The tour can host just a handful of people. Larger groups can be split into multiple tours to accommodate the space and time available.
Analysis: While similar first-person interpretive cemetery tours usually focus on the Halloween holiday, the Strolling with the Spirits' unique themed approach offers the potential to host a tour at any time through-

out the year. This allows the museum to capitalize on community interest generated by events and anniversaries, both local and national, and helps to justify the high time commitment the program requires. Museums interested in duplicating this program may want to consider the scheduling flexibility this themed approach offers early in the planning stage.

Veterans Day Program

Moody Museum, Taylor, Texas
Historic Site
Community Exhibit/Event
   Target Audience: Community veterans and their families
   Attendance: 50–100 people
   Overview: Every year, the Moody Museum invites community veterans and their families to celebrate Veterans Day at the museum. Each veteran is encouraged to submit a shadowbox or other military service memorabilia for temporary display in a community exhibit housed at the museum. Shadowboxes are made available to those who don't have one. The event includes the community exhibit, a flag-raising ceremony, a guest speaker, and refreshments.
   Budget: $100
   Interpretive Components: ★★ Interpretation is minimal for each shadowbox. Most interpretive information is shared through the guest speaker.
   Staff Time Requirements: ~20 hours. Much of the staff time requirement is devoted to contacting veterans and their families. Marketing is also included in this time.
   Audience Time Requirements: ~2 hours. Most attendees spend about two hours at the museum to hear the guest speaker, enjoy some refreshments, and explore the community exhibit.
   Scalability: ★★★★ This event can be scaled larger or smaller by simply adjusting the number of veterans invited to participate. The program can even be themed by war to further affect the scale.
   Analysis: The Moody Museum's Veterans' Day event encourages local veterans to contribute to programming components through submitting personal stories, objects, and documents to be shared in the community exhibit. This establishes participants as equal interpretive partners and offers the museum the chance to recognize the value of veterans' experiences in the context of the museum space. Opening the program to include these pieces extends exhibit information beyond the museum's collection and invites community members to share their own personal histories. This offers the opportunity to expand the museum's archival collection while building local support for museum efforts.

Credit: Moody Museum

Figure 5.18 Taylor native and Vietnam veteran Charles Nowlin speaks to the
assembled crowd at the Moody Museum's annual Veterans Day observance

Six-Week Spotlight

Haines Sheldon Museum, Haines, Alaska
History/Art Museum
Community Exhibit

Target Audience: Local visual artists

Attendance: More than 200 people

Overview: Every year, the Haines Sheldon Museum hosts a community exhibit of curated visual art by local artists and craftspeople. After a detailed application and acceptance process, artists are responsible for writing exhibit text, installing their pieces, and providing opening reception refreshments. The exhibit is open to the public for six weeks. During this time, the museum provides programming and in-gallery activities that correspond to the pieces on display.

Budget: $100

Interpretive Components: ★★★ All exhibit interpretive text is provided by the artists. Additional interpretation is included through the art-centered museum programming run while the exhibit is open.

Staff Time Requirements: ~25 hours. Staff time can vary, depending on how much assistance exhibiting artists require. The museum does provide marketing, printing materials for labels and wall text, and installation and dismantling assistance.

Audience Time Requirements: Flexible. Because the exhibit is open to the public, visitors are welcome to visit any time during the museum's open hours.

Scalability: ★★★★ The Six-Week Spotlight can be as big or as small as the space allows. It can highlight the work of a single artist, or it can include several pieces from multiple artists.

Analysis: Opening museum space to display local collections of artists' work can be a unique opportunity to expose museum visitors to the variety in their community and the museum's role in it. By further relinquishing much of the exhibiting responsibilities (e.g., text, installation, label mounting), the museum is able to dually host an exhibit with little maintenance while helping introduce artists to the exhibit process. Still, the Haines Sheldon Museum proves that giving up much of the responsibility does not mean settling for a subpar exhibit. Quality can be maintained through an extensive application process and by reviewing all text and installation pieces before the exhibit opens.

While the Six-Week Spotlight focuses on local artists, the community exhibit program model can be adapted to compliment any museum collection. Personal historic collections, wildlife photography, and local crafts could each find their way into similar exhibits. Museums looking to add this to their programming plan must explore ways to incorporate noncollection items while working to give up interpretive responsibilities—all without relinquishing museum exhibit best practices.

Victorian Tea Fundraiser

Latah County Historical Society, Moscow, Idaho
History Museum/Historic House
Event
   Target Audience: Multigeneration audience
   Attendance: 50–100 people
   Overview: The Victorian Tea Fundraiser is a volunteer-driven, ticketed meal event held in the McConnell Mansion, a historic house museum. Volunteers provide, prepare, and serve a multicourse luncheon using traditional Victorian high tea dishes and etiquette. Apple juice is made available for younger attendees. Participants are encouraged to immerse themselves in the experience as interpretation on Victorian manners is provided for each course. They are even invited to dress for the occasion. Following the meal, guests are led on a tour through the historic site.
   Budget: $100
   Interpretive Components: ★★★ Victorian-era manners and dinner etiquette are provided during the meal, and guests are given a tour of the historic house to explore the Victorian home.
   Staff Time Requirements: ~20 hours. Staff time includes planning the event, managing ticket sales, day-of preparation, running the event, and cleanup.
   Audience Time Requirements: 2 hours. This includes both the luncheon and the following tour.
   Scalability: ★★★ This event is wholly dependent on a strong volunteer base willing to donate the food and to prepare and serve it. The number of volunteers informs the number of guests they can serve. This is in addition to any space limitations.
   Analysis: While serving food in recognized exhibit spaces can make many museums nervous, the potential for creating a controlled, immersive atmosphere to build a unique experiential program should be acknowledged. Meticulously planning the menu and deliberately hosting the meal in specific spaces can subtly mitigate potential issues and contain any complications that may arise. By addressing these concerns before they become problems, the Latah County Historical Society is able to provide a singular event designed to surround and engage participants through experiential learning. Museums willing to explore this programming setting can create similar programmatic success.

Yule Log Hunt

Tread of Pioneers Museum, Steamboat Springs, Colorado
History Museum
Off-Site
    Target Audience: Local community audience
    Attendance: More than 200 people

Figure 5.19 Yule Log Hunt with the Tread of Pioneers Museum

Overview: Each year, the Tread of Pioneers Museum hides a large yule log for community members to search for in a large-scale treasure hunt. Community members must decode 10 riddles to find the log and win donated prizes. Each riddle describes a different historic location in town and is advertised in the local newspaper, online, and on local radio stations. The hunt begins at the previous year's hiding spot and leads participants throughout the community. Multiple winners find the log each year.
    Budget: $100
    Interpretive Components: ★★★ While interpretation is not a priority, participants must learn about and be familiar with local history and sometimes holiday traditions to answer each riddle.
    Staff Time Requirements: ~16 hours. Staff select the hiding place, write the riddles, and disseminate the clues.
    Audience Time Requirements: Variable. Community participants may take a few minutes or several hours to answer each riddle before finding the yule log.
    Scalability: ★★★★★ This community scavenger hunt encourages all residents and visitors to play. Participants can access the clues and sites at any time, allowing an untold number of people to take part.
    Analysis: The Yule Log Hunt invites the entire community to take part in a themed museum-led program that involves participants in learning

local history. Motivated by prizes, they are able to explore historic connections to contemporary sites in their bid to be the first to find the yule log. In this way, the museum is able to host a program that educates and engages while advancing their community-centered goals. Any museum willing to hide the log (or other object) and write and post the riddles could realistically adapt this program model.

6

Adapting, Expanding, and Implementing Museum Programs

Museum programs are a cornerstone to museum success. Formally planned visitor interactions provide meaningful engagement; encourage deeper understandings; and establish our organizations as places for fun, inspirational, and educational experiences—a place worthy of audience time. While program success can vary by museum type, location, and target audience, one thing is consistent: Establishing successful museum programs takes considerable time and effort, but it doesn't have to take a lot of money.

Many times, a lack of resources can be incredibly discouraging as we are forced to prioritize our activities. But programming efforts do not have to be sacrificed under new budget focuses. Instead, they can be continued with careful planning and dedication. The programs highlighted in this publication are a testament to the innovative experiences museums are producing with little money but loads of determination and ingenuity. They serve as a model for what can happen in similar situations. They can be adapted to fit different museum types, expanded to meet organizational goals, and implemented to satisfy community needs.

While there are numerous components to planning, implementing, and administering an effective program, these can be broken into smaller, manageable steps: identifying audience needs, assessing available resources, planning the program, determining desired goals and objectives, marketing, and evaluating success (see appendix C).

IDENTIFYING AUDIENCE NEEDS

Museums are for everyone, but planning programs for the general public is problematic. This approach generally puts the program's importance solely on what the museum wants; it is based solely on museum assumptions. It often does not take audience needs and expectations into account. Is the audience made up of school-age children? Teens? Adults? Or a cross-generational mix? Are they from the local community and familiar with the facility, or are they first-time visitors? Do they have special needs and unique requirements that must be met to adequately experience the museum? To be successful, the program must meet the demands and needs of its participants. A program's audience must be narrowed and targeted to ensure that program components match audience expectations.

To rightly identify what a program audience needs, museums must define the role the program is to play. Is the program intended to address a problem? Will it provide a needed service? Does it engage the audience with the museum's mission? Is it simply educational? Fun? Inspirational? What should participants do, feel, or think afterward? Often, we assume we already have the answers and attempt to address these programs without ever incorporating our audience, but this is a mistake. Successful museum programs are designed to fit a specific audience void and should be defined by the audience themselves. To do this, we must be willing to talk with our participant community, and we must be willing to listen and apply what we learn. Museum visitors know what they want, and they are willing to share when they know someone is listening.

Comments from potential program audiences can be gained through surveys, questionnaires, and simple face-to-face conversations, but there are other avenues to help define a program's target group. Evaluating local community service needs through economic development studies, local school performance ratings, and community comment boards are all ways to narrow the potential needs and experiences that can be met through museum programs.

ASSESSING AVAILABLE RESOURCES

All museums must operate within their available staffing, space, material, and financial resources. Defining which of those resources are available for a new program is vital to establishing an engaging and sustainable effort. Every program must operate within an established budget, even if that budget is $0. But there are resources available to us that have nothing to do with our museums' bank accounts. Taking an accurate inventory of on-site materials can define programmatic activities. Buying in bulk can be the difference between a single-year program and a recurring annual event. Establishing and tracking community networks of individuals and businesses willing to donate time, money, and materials requires legwork and effort, but it can yield vital results. Nurturing a dedicated and invested volunteer base can make logistically impossible events seem easy. These resources are available to every museum in differing capacities, and they create the foundation for community-supported programming efforts.

PLANNING THE PROGRAM

Program Selection

Knowing our audience and our resources is only the first step in developing a museum program. Selecting and planning the program takes up most of the effort associated with programming advancement. When developing a programming theme or idea, it is important to be willing to explore the unexpected. Unexpected perspectives, spaces, voices, and even controversies capture audiences' attention and engages their imaginations. Both are necessary to bring them back into the museum space. We must avoid tradition; "we've always done it this way" or "we've never done it that way" are traps that will bog down any programming effort. Museum programs should offer a fresh approach to our missions and our collections.

We should be willing to try many different things without becoming tied to any one program or program type. Organizations that aren't afraid to fail are more likely to find that programming niche their audience craves, all while still fitting within their missions, spaces, and resources.

One notable thing about the museum field is our willingness to share ideas, experiences, and concepts. Rarely are museum professionals unlikely to pass on the fine details of a particular program. This means we can freely adapt programs from one facility to another. If the Carbon County Museum's Rawlins History Hunt fits another museum's needs, then they are free to adapt its features, and they can reach out to Carbon County Museum with questions (see textbox 6.1). If a facility wants to plan their own Pioneer Garden but is unsure how to schedule youth volunteers, then they are welcome to contact the Grand Encampment Museum for advice. This is a unique feature of the museum field and one that isn't utilized enough.

Creating a Program Plan

Creating a written program plan is an important part of successful museum programming. Not only does the plan help finalize program components, but it also serves as a blueprint for museum staff to repeat the program in subsequent iterations and can be vital against failure during staff turnover. The plan should outline who will do what in relation

---

ADAPTING RAWLINS HISTORY HUNT

The Rawlins History Hunt is a school program for teenagers that pairs an on-site museum visit with a community scavenger hunt to identify historic downtown locations. It gives participants controlled autonomy, encourages social collaboration, and even incorporates technology to earn appropriate credit. But how can it be adapted for a different facility, such as an art museum?

To best adjust the program, the components must be analyzed to determine what can be kept and what must be changed. In this instance, the instructional museum visit to orient students to the activity can be kept. However, instead of historic interpretation, chosen artistic themes, processes, or artists can be substituted. Students can still travel downtown to search and apply this information, but instead of looking for specific buildings or locations, now they can look for visual designs or architectural features. For example, students can observe the applications of color theory in the museum galleries and then provide an example of it in business logos or signage designs. Or perhaps students can make a study of landscape sketches and then be charged with photographing a duplicate angle or view during their downtown visit.

While the basic nature of the Rawlins History Hunt program has been kept—for example, instructional trips to the museum paired with applied visits to a second location—the content has been adjusted to fit the purview and mission of a differing institution, in this case, an art museum.

---

to specific program responsibilities, which resources it requires, and an overall time line for program development and implementation.

When creating a program plan, museums should include the program's purpose, step-by-step instructions, resources, and proposed goals and objectives (discussed in the next section). It should also outline the specific program content, instructional design, timing, and projected cost. Having these details formalized in writing solidifies the program's role within the museum's overall programming and strategic plans.

While this discussion has included the general foundation components of a museum program, it is important to include the finer details of the program in the written plan. Components like location options, budget, and evaluations help to further establish the program and document its viability for continuing (for a program plan checklist, see appendix B).

If the program is being adapted from another museum facility, a program plan is all the more important. In addition to components discussed previously, it should also note which pieces need to be altered to fit the new museum's goals. What needs to be changed? What needs to be removed? What needs to be added? Documenting these portions further marks the program's evolution.

DETERMINING DESIRED GOALS AND OBJECTIVES

When developing museum programs, it is vital to establish goals and objectives as part of the programming plan. What exactly do we want the program to accomplish? What do we want people to do after participating in the program? It is important to note that goals and objectives are different though complementary pieces. Goals are what we want to *happen* as a result of the program. They are not necessarily audience related, and they usually include some type of measurable component. Objectives are what you want the audience to *do* as a result of the program. They tend to be behavioral. For example, the Latah County Historical Society's Victorian Tea Fundraiser may have a goal of raising $10,000 for the organization. To achieve this, their objective may be to have 100 percent of attendees donate. Each statement is a separate piece of a united purpose born from a single program.

MARKETING

Marketing is perhaps the most important part of establishing a successful museum program. There is no program without an audience, and there is no audience without marketing. As discussed in chapter 1, marketing in the digital age requires planning, but it can be done with little to no financial investment. Most importantly, remember to know who the marketing is for so efforts can be made to identify the best ways to reach that group. This harkens back to identifying the target audience, who they are, what they want, and what they need.

EVALUATING SUCCESS

Perhaps the most overlooked aspect of creating successful museum programs is evaluation. Gathering audience feedback is one of the most dependable measures of program success, but it is so often neglected. Evaluation results help us to make data-informed decisions to distribute time and resources. It helps establish whether we're meeting community needs, and it can even determine whether a program should continue. Evaluations provide the information for us to know why we do what we do and informs how we should do it.

Evaluations should be done early and often. Early, or formative, evaluations can inform how a program is developed. Remedial evaluations occur while the program is active and helps identify changes or adjustments that need to be made to keep the program in line with its purpose, objectives, and the museum's mission. Summative evaluations are conducted when a program has completed and is no longer on the museum schedule. These evaluations can document the overall success, or lack thereof, of a program and inform whether it should be revisited in the future.

The information gained through these evaluations not only updates the museum on how the program went, but it also can apprise granting agencies and donors on the program's impact, solidifying supportive relationships between the museum and these outside agencies.

It is important to note that not every implemented museum program will work for that museum's audience, goals, and budget. Not every program will be a success. The danger lies in continuing a program even when it doesn't meet the organization's needs. We must be willing to shut it down if necessary. Don't lean on a dead or dying program. It will drain our resources, our time, and our motivation.

In short, we must know when to cut our losses. Know exactly how long the program can wait to see a return (hence the importance of those goals and outcomes). At what point does the program cost too much per audience member? When does it take too much staff time when only a handful of participants benefit? Not every program will work for every audience, and while we need to be willing to try new programming options, we must also be willing to cut them when they fail to meet our needs.

Museums are amazing, and museum professionals make it so. Audiences continue to seek meaningful and unexpected experiences, and museum programming efforts continue to meet these needs without overextending resources. With programs like the Cape Fear Museum's Sewing and Circuits activity or the Conrad-Cadwell House Museum's Twilight Tours, it is evident that we make these programs work, and we make them work on a dime.

APPENDIX A

Project Contributors

Agecroft Hall
4305 Sulgrave Rd.
Richmond, VA 23221
agecrofthall.com

Alutiiq Museum and Archaeology
   Repository
215 Mission Rd.
Kodiak, Alaska 99615
alutiiqmuseum.org

Amherst Historical Society
67 Amity St.
Amherst, MA 01002
amhersthistory.org

Aurora Fossil Museum Foundation
400 Main St.
Aurora, NC 27806
aurorafossilmuseum.org

Battle of Franklin Trust
1345 Eastern Flank Cir.
Franklin, TN 37064
boft.org

Blanden Art Museum
920 3rd Ave. S
Fort Dodge, IA 50501
blanden.org

Brigham City Museum of Art and
   History
24 N 300 W
Brigham City, UT 84302
brighamcity.utah.gov/museum.htm

Brucemore, Inc.
2160 Linden Dr. SE
Cedar Rapids, IA 52403
brucemore.org

Bullock Texas State History Museum
1800 Congress Ave.
Austin, TX 78701
thestoryoftexas.com

Cape Fear Museum
814 Market St.
Wilmington, NC 28401
capefearmuseum.org

Carbon County Museum
904 W. Walnut
Rawlins, WY 82301
carboncountymuseum.org

Cass County Historical Society
1351 W. Main Ave.
West Fargo, ND 58078
cchsmo.org

Chieftains Museum/Major Ridge
   Home
501 Riverside Pkwy NE
Rome, GA 30161
chieftainsmuseum.org

Children's Museum of Pittsburgh
10 Children's Way
Pittsburgh, PA 15212
pittsburghkids.org

Children's Museum of Richmond
2626 W Broad St.
Richmond, VA 23220
c-mor.org

City of Raleigh Museum
220 Fayetteville St.
Raleigh, NC 27601
cityofraleighmuseum.org

Codington County Heritage Museum
27 1st Ave. SE
Watertown, SD 57201
cchsmuseum.org

Concord Museum
200 Lexington Rd.
Concord, MA 01742
concordmuseum.org

Conrad-Caldwell House Museum
1402 St. James Ct.
Louisville, KY 40208
conrad-caldwell.org

Daviess County Historical Society
   Museum
212 E Main St.
Washington, IN 47501
daviesscountyhistory.net

Evansville African American Museum
579 S Garvin St.
Evansville, IN 47713
evansvilleaamuseum.wordpress.com

Friends of the Pound House
   Foundation
570 Founders Park Rd.
Dripping Springs, TX 78620
drpoundhistoricalfarmstead.org

Gamble House
4 Westmoreland Pl.
Pasadena, CA 91103
gamblehouse.org

Georgia Museum of Art
90 Carlton St.
Athens, GA 30602
georgiamuseum.org

German American Heritage Center
712 W 2nd St.
Davenport, IA 52802
gahc.org

The Grace Museum
102 Cypress St.
Abilene, TX 79601
thegracemuseum.org

Grand Encampment Museum
807 Barnett Ave.
Encampment, WY 82325
gemuseum.com

Grout Museum District
503 South St.
Waterloo, IA 50701
groutmuseumdistrict.org

Haines Sheldon Museum
11 Main St.
Haines, AK 99827
sheldonmuseum.org

Harn Museum of Art
3259 Hull Rd.
Gainesville, FL 32611
harn.ufl.edu

Historical Museum at Ft. Missoula
3400 Captain Rawn Way
Missoula, MT 59804
fortmissoulamuseum.org

History Colorado Center
1200 N Broadway
Denver, CO 80203
historycolorado.org

Indiana State Museum and Historic
   Sites
650 W Washington St.
Indianapolis, IN 46204
indianamuseum.org

International Spy Museum
800 F St. NW
Washington, DC 20004
spymuseum.org

Japanese Cultural Center of Hawai'i
2454 S Beretania St.
Honolulu, HI 96826
jcch.org

Jeanerette Museum
500 Main St.
Jeanerette, LA 70544
jeanerettemuseum.com

Johnson County Jim Gatchell Memorial Museum
100 Fort St.
Buffalo, WY 82834
jimgatchell.com

Kenosha Public Museum
500 First Ave.
Kenosha, WI 53140
museums.kenosha.org

Lahaina Restoration Foundation
120 Dickenson St.
Lahaina, HI 96761
lahainarestoration.org

Latah County Historical Society
327 E 2nd St.
Moscow, ID 83843
latah.id.us

Lexington Historical Society
13 Depot Square
Lexington, MA 02420
lexingtonhistory.org

Mabee-Gerrer Museum of Art
1900 W MacArthur St.
Shawnee, OK 74804
mgmoa.org

Mai Wah Society and Museum
17 W Mercury St.
Butte, MT 59701
maiwah.org

Maine Historical Society
489 Congress St.
Portland, ME 04101
mainehistory.org

Marietta Museum of History
1 Depot St.
Marietta, GA 30060
mariettahistory.org

Marshall Steam Museum
3000 Creek Rd.
Yorklyn, DE 19736
auburneheights.org

Moody Museum
114 W 9th St.
Taylor, TX 76574
moodymuseum.com

Museum Center at 5ive Points
200 Inman St. E
Cleveland, TN 37311
museumcenter.org

Museum of American Printing House
  for the Blind
1839 Frankfort Ave.
Louisville, KY 40206
aph.org/museum

Museum of Indian Arts and Culture
710 Camino Lejo
Santa Fe, NM 87505
indianartsandculture.org

Museum of Latin American Art
628 Alamitos Ave.
Long Beach, CA 90802
molaa.org

Museum of People and Cultures at
  Brigham Young University
2201 N Canyon Rd.
Provo, UT 84604
mpc.byu.edu

Museum of Texas Tech University
Texas Tech University
3301 4th St.
Lubbock, TX 79415
www.depts.ttu.edu/museumttu

Museum of World Treasures
835 E 1st St. N
Wichita, KS 67202
worldtreasures.org

National Mining Hall of Fame and
  Museum
120 W. 9th St.
Leadville, CO 80461
mininghalloffame.org

National Museum of Women in the
  Arts
1250 New York Ave. NW
Washington, DC 20005
nmwa.org

Neon Museum
770 N Las Vegas Blvd.
Las Vegas, NV 89101
neonmuseum.org

Oklahoma History Center
800 Nazih Zuhdi Dr.
Oklahoma City, OK 73105
okhistory.org/historycenter

Penn Museum
3260 South St.
Philadelphia, PA 19104
penn.museum

Rutherford B. Hayes Presidential Library and Museum
Spiegel Grove
Fremont, OH 43420
rbhayes.org

Shadows-on-the-Teche
317 E Main St.
New Iberia, LA 70560
shadowsontheteche.org

Shelburne Museum
6000 Shelburne Rd.
Shelburne, VT 05482
shelburnemuseum.org

Shenandoah Valley Discovery
  Museum
19 W. Cork St.
Winchester, VA 22601
discoverymuseum.net

Skirball Cultural Center
2701 N Sepulveda Blvd.
Los Angeles, CA 90049
skirball.org

South County History Center
2636 Kingstown Rd.
Kingston, RI 02881
southcountyhistorycenter.org

Tallahassee Museum
3945 Museum Rd.
Tallahassee, FL 32310
tallahasseemuseum.org

Tread of Pioneers Museums
800 Oak St.
Steamboat Springs, CO 80477
treadofpioneers.org

UO Museum of Natural and Cultural
  History
1680 E 15th Ave.
Eugene, OR 97401
natural-history.uoregon.edu

US Naval Undersea Museum
1 Garnett Way
Keyport, WA 98345
navalunderseamuseum.org

Victoria Mansion
109 Danforth St.
Portland, ME 04101
victoriamansion.org

Western Spirit: Scottsdale's Museum
  of the West
3830 N. Marshall Way
Scottsdale, AZ 85251
scottsdalemuseumwest.org

White River Museum and Mary Olson
  Farm
918 H St. SE
Auburn, WA 98002
wrvmuseum.org

Williams College Museum of Art
15 Lawrence Hall Dr., No. 2
Williamstown, MA 01267
wcma.williams.edu

Wyoming Dinosaur Center
110 Carter Ranch Rd.
Thermopolis, WY 82443
wyodino.org

APPENDIX B

Program Planning Checklist

Developing, implementing, and managing a new program can be challenging and time consuming. Having a good program plan can mitigate any issues that may arise throughout the process. Use the checklist here to help establish a successful museum program.

- ☐ Identify program purpose, goals, and objectives.
- ☐ Determine budget.
- ☐ Develop central theme, idea, or concept.
- ☐ Plan program progression (what happens when?).
- ☐ Identify resources (needed and on-site, including outside staff).
- ☐ Reassess budget.
- ☐ Adjust program plan as needed.
- ☐ Develop marketing components.
- ☐ Prepare and test program.
- ☐ Adjust program as needed.
- ☐ Submit marketing to planned media outlets.
- ☐ Launch program.
- ☐ Revisit program plan periodically for evaluation and adjustment.

Appendix C

Developing a Museum Program: Sample Program Planning Worksheet

Program Title: Youth Tour Ambassadors
Target Audience (Who is the program for?): local youth, grades 4–12
Budget: $50
Program Goal(s) (Why are you doing the program?): to increase youth involvement with the museum
Program Objective(s) (What do you want the audience to do?): develop trained, dedicated group of volunteers available to help meet museum project needs
Resources/Materials: paper, markers, computer or tablet (already have), small archival gloves, snacks for concluding event
Program Plan (What will happen during the program?): Participants will be required to volunteer a total of 20 hours over the summer for training and to gain experience. Responsibilities will include learning how to welcome visitors, designing a small exhibit using the Education Collection, cutting and filing birth and obituary notices, gallery cleaning, and other projects as available
Program Marketing (What is the best marketing medium[s] for your audience?): press release to local newspaper and radio, social media posts, newsletter announcements
Program Staff (Who will run the program?): Education and outreach coordinator, other staff depending on specific project needs
Program Logistics

- *Program Location (Where will the program be held? Does the capacity fit the program needs?):* museum building and grounds
- *Program Length (How long will the audience need to stay?):* 1- to 2-hour shifts, with a total of 20 hours required per volunteer

Appendix D

Developing a Museum Program: Blank Program Planning Worksheet

Program Title:

Target Audience (Who is the program for?):

Budget:

Program Goal(s) (Why are you doing the program?):

Program Objective(s) (What do you want the audience to do?):

Resources/Materials:

Program Plan (What will happen during the program?)

Program Marketing (What is the best marketing medium[s] for your audience?):

Program Staff (Who will run the program?):

Program Logistics

- *Program Location (Where will the program be held? Does the capacity fit the program needs?):*

- *Program Length (How long will the audience need to stay?):*

Index

Page references for figures are italicized.

activity-based program, *x*, 11-12, 19, 55, 80, 101, 140
advertising. *See* marketing
advertising plan, 5
after-hours, 52, 114, 115, 122, 123, 130, 144, 145
Agecroft Hall, 10, 14-15, 67, 77-78, 163
alcohol, 84, 97-98, 109-11, 111-12
Alutiiq Museum & Archaeology Repository, 116, 127-29, *128*, 163
    Meet the Artist, 116, 127-29, *128*
Alzheimer's Association, 104
Amherst Historical Society, 115, 126-27, 163
    Flax: From Plant to Thread, 115, 126-27
    Simeon Strong House, 126
architecture, 55, 100, 144, 147, 148, *160*
art museum, 16, 19, 22, 42, 56, 68, 70, 72, 79, 86, 89, 90, 101, 108, 117, 121, 127, 129, 133, 137, 138, 150, 152
artist, 43, 52, 57, 63, 72, 80, 87, 89, 90, 104, 118, 121-22, 127-*28*, 129, 153, *160*
audience needs, 157-158
Aurora Fossil Museum Foundation, *140*-41, 163
autism, 137-138

Battle of Franklin Trust, 82, 85-86, 163
    Carton House, 86

Carter House, 86
beer. *See* alcohol
behind-the-scenes, 68, 82, 89, 92, 94, 99, 100, 114, 134, 145, 147
Blanden Art Museum, 114, *121*-22, 163
Bohl, J. David, *25*
book club, 94-95
Brigham City Museum of Art & History, 82, 86-87, 163
    Behind the Seams, 82, 86-87
Brucemore, Inc., *144*-45, 163
Bullock Texas State History Museum, 83, 95-97, *96*, 163
    Discovering History through Artifacts, 83, 95-97, *96*

Cape Fear Museum, 10, 43-44, 46-48, *47*, 82, 93-94, 163
    CuraTOURial, 82, 93-94
    Sewing & Circuits, 10, 46, *47*, 48, 162
    Summer Pop-Ups, 43-44
Carbon County Museum, 13-14, *41*-42, 74-75, 159, *160*, 163
    Rawlins History Hunt, 74-75, 159, *160*
    Youth Tour Ambassadors, 13-14, *41*-42
Carson, Buss, 124
Carson Family Western Show, 124
Carson, Nichole Bonilla, 124
Cass County Historical Society, 29-30, 52-53, 84, 94-95, 163
    Bonnet Book Club, 84, 94-95

Fall History Day, 29-30
    Teddy Bear Tea, 52-53
Cheshire, Bethany, *137*
Chieftains Museum, *146-47*, 164
children's museum, 15, 26, 30, 50, 80
Children's Museum of Pittsburgh, 12,
    30-31, 67, 68, 80, 164
Children's Museum of Richmond, 11,
    26-27, 164
    Special Nights for Special Needs,
    11, 26-27
City of Raleigh Museum, *51-52*, 164
class (scheduled), 83
Codington County Heritage Museum,
    84, 90-92, *91*, 164
    History Club, 84, 90-92, *91*
College of Southern Nevada
    Planetarium, 138
Concord Museum, 84, 109-11, *110*, 164
    Father's Day Beer Talk & Tasting,
    84, 109-11, *110*
Conrad-Caldwell House Museum, 114,
    122-23, 162, 164
    Twilight Tours, 114, 122-23, 162
contest, *xi*, 67, 79
Cooper, Gary, 125
culture center, 46, 53, 56, 61, 78, 102,
    107, 119, 125, 127, 137, 147

Daviess County Historical Society
    Museum, 10, 13, 18-19, 35-36, 164
    Fourth Grade Trips, 10, 18-19
    Kids Klub, 13, 35-36
dementia. *See* memory loss
demonstration, *xi*, 115, 126, 127, 134
docent. *See* volunteer

elderly. *See* senior citizen
evaluation, 5, 93, 109, 158, 160, 161-162
    formative, 162
    marketing, 5
    remedial, 162
    summative, 162
Evansville African American Museum,
    10-11, 56-57, 83, 102-3, 164
    Building Bridges Forum, 83, 102-3

Family Painting Workshop, 10-11,
    56-57
event, *xi*, 2, 11, 16, 21, 29, 52, 53, 83-84,
    107, 109, 111, 114-15, 121, 125, 142,
    151, 154
exhibit, *x*, 2, *3*, *4*, *5*, 13, 22, 26, 28, 31,
    36, 42, 44, 45, 62, 70, 73, 78, 79, 81,
    82, 86, 87, 89, 94, 96, 101, 105, 107,
    108, 110, 125, 129, 134-35, 145, 148
    community, *x*, 33, 115-16, 127, 151,
    152

Floyd County Master Gardeners, 147
Friends of the Pound House
    Foundation, 10, 48-49, 164
    Canning Creations, 10, 48-49

gallery guide. *See* volunteer
Gamble House, 82, *99-100*, 164
    Behind the Velvet Ropes, 82, *99-100*
Generation Z, 65
Georgia Museum of Art, 66, 68-70, *69*,
    164
    Snapchat, 66, 68-70, *69*
German American Heritage Center,
    114, 125-26, 164
    How to Make Sauerkraut, 114, 125-
    26
Grace Museum, 12, 19-21, *20*, 164
    Pop-Up Make N'Take, 12, 19-21, *20*
Grand Encampment Museum, 13, 14,
    33-35, *34*, 159, 164
    Pioneer Garden, 13, 14, 33-35, *34*,
    159
Grout Museum District, 114, 115, 133-
    34, 150-51, 164
    Star Parties, 115, 133-34
    Strolling with the Spirits, 114, 150-
    51

Haines Sheldon Museum, 116, 152-53,
    164
    Six-Week Spotlight, 116, 152-53
Hala, Jackie, *130*
hands-on learning, 9, 10, 12, 14, 18, 20,
    21, 29, 33, 34, 36, 39, 47, 56, 59, 77,

83, 89, 97, 98, 101, 108, 111, 113, 117, 118, 126, 127, 135, 136, 141, 145-47
See also participatory learning
Harn Museum of Art, 67, 79, 164
    Words on Canvas, 67, 79
Hashknife Pony Express, 11, 16
Henricus Historical Park, 14
historic house, 14, 24, 77, 99, 122, 154
historic site, 36, 38, 45, 48, 57, 73, 85, 99, 106, 130, 142, 146, 144, 151
Historical Museum at Fort Missoula, 10, 36-37, 165
    Artifact Detective & Exhibit Label Workshop, 10, 36-37
History Colorado Center, 27-28, 85, 104-5, 114, 145-46, 165
    Historical Craft Society, 114, 145-46
Preschool Story Time, 27-28
SPARK!, 85, 104-5
history museum, 16, 18, 19, 21, 22, 27, 29, 31-33, 35, 36, 38, 39, 41, 43-46, 51, 52, 55,61, 63, 74, 75, 86, 87, 90-95, 97, 98, 100-104, 106-9, 111, 118, 124-27, 129, 131, 133, 134, 137, 138, 145-48, 150, 152, 154
homeschool, 29
Houghton, Dr. Vince, 119

in-gallery program, *xi*, 2, 24, 27, 30, 39, 43, 44, 50, 61, 101, 129, 137, 148
Indiana State Museum & Historic Sites, 115, *134-35*, 165
    Museum Collection Protection, 115, *134-35*
instructional design, 160
International Spy Museum, *118-19*, 165
    Spycast, *118-19*
interpretation, x, 3, 9

Japanese Cultural Center of Hawai'i, 119-21, *120*, 165
    Japanese Name Interpretation Workshop, 119-21, *120*
Jeanerette Museum, 83, 106, 165
    History Talks, 83, 106

Johnson County Jim Gatchell Memorial Museum, 10, 32-33, 114, 131-32, *132*, 165
    Echoes of the Past Cemetery Tour, 114, 131-33, *132*
    Neighborhoods, 10, *32-33*
Jordan, Jim, 11, *21-22*

Kenosha Public Museum, 42-43, 116, 117-18, 165
    Darwin Day, 42-43
    Women in Science, 116, 117-18
King County Library System, 45

Lahaina Restoration Foundation, 114, *130-31*, 165
    Baldwin Home Candlelight Tour, 114, *130-31*
Las Vegas Astronomical Society, 138
Latah County Historical Society, 85, 98-99, 154, 161, 165
    Pastimes & Memories, 85, 98-99
    Victorian Tea Fundraiser, 154, 161
lecture, *xi*, 82-83, 87-88, 92-93, 102, 106, 111, 124, 135
Lexington Historical Society, 10, *38-39*, 165
    Children's Battle of Lexington Reenactment, 10, *38-39*
library, 21, 98, 141

Mabee-Gerrer Museum of Art, 10, 22-24, *23*, 165
    Start with Art, 10, 22-24, *23*
Mai Wah Society, 114, 147-48, 165
    Below the Scenes, 114, 147-48
Maine Historical Society, 84, 97-98, 165
    Beer in the Garden, 84, 97-98
Major Ridge Home, *146*
makerspace, 12, 30, 67, 80
marketing, ix-xi, 16, 42, 52, 59, 63, 76, 86, 88, 109, 120, 132, 157, 161, 169, 171, 173
    digital, 5-6
Marietta Museum of History, 12-13, 31, 84, 103-4, 165

Museum of Mice Toddler Tour,
	12-13, 31
	Remember When Club, 84, 103-4
Marshall Steam Museum, 82, 92-*93*,
	165
	Evening at the Museum, 82, 92-*93*
Mary Olson Farm, 12, 45-46, 167
McConnell Mansion, 154
memory loss, 85-86, 104-*5*, 138
Millennial, 65
mission statement, 2-3, 4, 15, 17, 39,
	54-55, 119, 148, 158, 159, 160, 162
Moody Museum, 11, 57-59, *58*, 115,
	116, 142-44, *143*, 151-52, 165
Panel Discussion on Race & Ethnicity,
	115, 142-44, *143*
Veterans Day, 116, 151-*52*
Victorian Christmas, 11, 57-59, *58*
multidisciplinary, 10, 18, 22, 33, 35, 41,
	43, 46, 63, 64, 77, 78, 96
Museum Center at 5ive Points, 84, 111-
	12, 114, 125, 165
	History Happy Hour, 84, 111-*12*
	Sergeant York Film Viewing, 114,
	125
Museum of Indian Arts & Crafts, 85,
	90, 166
	Let's Take a Look, 85, 90
Museum of Latin American Art, 66,
	72-73, 166
	Tumblr, 66, 72-73
Museum of Natural & Cultural
	History (University of Oregon), 13,
	44-45, 167
	Little Wonders, 13, 44-45
Museum of Peoples and Cultures at
	BYU, *61*-62, 84, 107, 166
	Mornings at the Museum, *61*-62
	Culture Me Mine Date Night, 84,
	107
Museum of Texas Tech University,
	117, *137*-38, 166
	Art with Emotion, 117, *137*-38
Museum of the American Printing
	House for the Blind, 18, 166
	Braille for the Sighted, 18

Museum of World Treasures, 82, 85,
	108-9, 166
	Unlocking the Stories, 82, 85, *108*-9
museum service program, 85, 90

National Constitution Center, 1
National Mining Hall of Fame &
	Museum, 12, *55*-56, 166
	Gold Panning, 12, *55*-56
National Museum of Women in the
	Arts, 82, 89, 166
	Member Preview Day, 82, 89
Neely Mansion, 12, 45-46
Neon Museum, 83, 101-102, 115, 138-
	39, 166
	Hot Yoga, 83, 101-102
	Stars & Stardust, 115, 138-*39*
Nowlin, Charlie, *152*

O'Bryan, Julia, *58*
object-based learning, 96-97
off-site, *xi*, 59 98, 131, 135, 140, 154
Oklahoma History Center, 116, 148-50,
	149, 166
	Hands-On History Carts, 116, 148-
	50, *149*
open house, *xi*, 11, 15, 26, 29, 42, 50,
	51, 57, 81-82, 85, 89, 90, 97, 117, 133,
	138
operations (museum), 2, 94
oral history, *xi*, 98-99, 103-4
outdoor program, 13, 115
outreach, 116

panel discussion, 83, 88, 102-3, 115,
	142, *143*
participatory learning, 44
	See also hands-on learning
partnership, *xi*, 6-7, 11, 12, 14, 15, 16,
	17, 21, 24, 27, 30, 45, 55, 63, 73, 84,
	98, 101, 104, 108, 109, 111, 115, 127,
	133, 138, 142, 146
Penn Museum, 66, 75-77, *76*, 166
	Teen Summer Internships, 66,
	75-77, *76*
performance art, 19, 52, 77, 78, 133,
	121-22

perspective, 1, 9, 24, 43, 62, 78, 79, 82, 83, 88, 94, 101, 103-4, 106, 112, 114, 122, 131, 143, 144, 145, 150, 159
podcast, *xi*, 117, 118-119
pop-up program. *See* activity-based program
preschool program, 12-13, 31, 44, 50, 54
primary source, 67, 73-74
program
    checklist, 169
    children, 9
    definition of, *4*, 5
    goal, 160-61
objective, 160-62
    program plan, 157, 159-61
    purpose of, *3*, 162
selection, 159
worksheet, 171, 173

Rapscallion Brewery of Acton, 109
relevance, 143
resources, 3, 5-7, 157, 158-159, 160, 162
Rutherford B. Hayes Presidential Library & Museum, 11, *21-22, 141-42*, 166
    Learning about YOUR Past, *141*-42
    President's Day Event, 11, *21-22*

school program, *xi*, 2, 9-10, 14, 18, 22, 32, 36, 38, 67, 74, 77
science museum, 39, 42, 43, 44, 46, 59, 93, 100, 117, 133, 135, 137, 140, 150
senior citizens, 98-99, 100-101, 104-5
senior program, 84-85, 98-99, 100-101, 103-4, 104-5
Shadows-on-the-Teche, 67, 73-74, 166
Shelburne Museum, 116, 129-30, 166
    1 in 10, 116, 129-30
Shenandoah University
    nursing program, 11, 15
Shenandoah Valley Discovery Museum, 11, 13, 15-16, 50, 166
    Healthy Fridays, 11, 15-16
    Itty Bitty Mornings, 13, 50
Skirball Cultural Center, 12, 53-55, *54*, 66, 68, 78-79, 166

Playdate, 12, 53-55, *54*
Teen Corps, 66, 68, 78-79
Snapchat, 66, 68, *69*, 70, 117
social club, *xi*, 13, 35, 80, 84, 91, 94, 103, 145
social issues, 102, 115
social media, *xi*, 5-6, 66, 68, 72, 117
    marketing with, 5-6
    program, 66, 68, 72
South County History Center, 83, 87-89, *88*, 166
    Palisades Mill, 83, 87-89, *88*
special needs, 6, 26-27, 104, 138, 158
STEAM, 40, 41
    See also multidisciplinary
story time, *xi*, 12, 24, 27, 30, 45
strategic plan, 160

Tallahassee Museum, 84, 100-101, 167
    Butter Making, 84, 100-101
teacher, 10, 23, 32, 33, 37, 77, 82, 83, 85-86, 95-97, 142
Tilden, Freeman, 9
tour, *xi*, 2, 31, 70, 73, 77, 82, 86, 93, 99, 108, 114, 122, 130, 131, 144, 147, 150
    school, 24, 77
Tread of Pioneers, 10, *63-64*, 116, 154-*55*, 167
    Lulie Crawford Wildflowers & Watercolors, 10, *63-64*
    Yule Log Hunt, 116, 154-*55*
Tumblr, 66, 72-73, 117

United States Naval Undersea Museum, 12, 39-41, *40*, 167
    Summer STEAM, 12, 39-41, *40*

veteran, 6, 103, 116, 150-51, *152*
Victoria Mansion, 12, 24-26, *25*, 167
    Stories on the Staircase, 12, 24-26, *25*
vision statement, 2-3
Visual Thinking Strategies (VTS), 24
volunteer, 29, 41-42, 70, 76, 79, 93, 95, 106, 114, 119, 120, 122, 123, 129, 130, 131-32, 147, 148-50, 154, 158-59

volunteer program, *xi*, 13, 41, 66, 70,
    75, 78
VTS. *See* Visual Thinking Strategies

walk-up program, 116
Wellstone, Paul, 1
Western Spirit, 11, 16-17, 124, 167
    Hashknife Pony Express Arrival,
    11, 16-17
    A Cowgirl's Legacy, 124
White River Valley Museum, 12, 45-46,
    167
    Bookmarks & Landmarks, Jr., 12,
    45-46

Williams College Museum of Art, 66,
    70-71, 167
    Student Choice, 66, 70-71
workshop program, *xi*, 10-11, 18, 36,
    46, 48, 56, 63, 73, 90, 95, 100, 102,
    104, 113-14, 119, 125, 137, 141, 145,
    146
Wright Tavern, 109
Wyoming Dinosaur Center, 10, 59-60,
    117, 135-36, 167
    Kids Dig, 10, 59-60
    Shovel Ready, 117, 135-36

About the Author

Lauren E. Hunley has spent more than 15 years in the museum field. After earning her master of arts in learning and visitor services in museums and galleries through Leicester University in England, she's worked for both small museums and national museum-service organizations. She is the education and outreach coordinator at Carbon County Museum in Rawlins, Wyoming. She also serves on the board of directors for the Mountain-Plains Museums Association and is the digital credential program chair. Lauren loves to discuss the museum field and the opportunities it offers. You can e-mail her at lauren.hunley@gmail.com.